EXPLANATION.
Stations or Forts
Salt Springs & Licks.
Towns.
Dwelling-houses & Mills.
Wigwams.
The dotted lines represent
Roads some Clear'd others
not.

While this Work shall live,
let this Inscription remain a Monument of
the Gratitude of the Author, to Col.º Dan.¹ Boon,
Levi Todd, & Ja.ˢ Harrod, Capt.ᵗ Chris.ᵗ Greenbeg
In.ᵗ Cowan, & W.ᵐ Kennedy Esq.ʳ of Kentucke: for
the distinguish'd Assistance, with which they have
honor'd him, in its Composition: & a testimony,
that it has recieved the Aprobation of those,
whom he justly Esteems, the best qualified to
Judge of its Merit.

INDIAN TERRITORY

Pecaway town

Old Chelicothe

Mingo Nation
live here

Paint Cr.

Natural Meadow

Little Miami

Big Indian Cr.

Sciotha River

Old Shawane
Town

Natural Meadow

FAYETTE

LICKING RIVER

Nth Fork

Fine Cane Land

Main Licking

the Blue licks
a fine salt spring

Upper Blue licks

COUNTY

Fine Cane

Abundance
of Cane

Riddle St.ⁿ

Hingston Fork

Elkhorn

Greenville

Lexington

Lee's-town

Col. Marshal's
Office

Bryan's

Stroud's

Col. Todd.

Boon's

RED RIVER

F-

Col. Boon's

Boonsburg

KENTUCKY

R-

Fine Cane
Bards Town.

Harrod
Town.

Dick's R.

LINCOLN

Blue lick

Craig's

Hanging Fork

COUNTY

COUNTY

Part of Cumberland Mountain

CUM-BER-LAND

KENTUCKY

KEN
A Pictorial

Principal Contributors: CHARLES L. ATCHER · EDWARD L. BOWEN · JACQUELINE BULL
RABEL J. BURDGE · GAYLE CARVER · KENNETH AND MARY CLARKE · A. LEE COLEMAN, JR.
HENRY H. CRAIG · JOE CREASON · W. JEROME CROUCH · J. CRAWFORD CROWE · HENRY G. CROWGEY
LEONARD P. CURRY · RICHARD B. DRAKE · CLEMENT EATON · JOSEPH A. ESTES · THOMAS P. FIELD
ELIZABETH D. GILBERT · MARY WILMA HARGREAVES · HENRY HARNED · LOWELL H. HARRISON
DANNY R. HATCHER · CHARLES F. HINDS · ALBERT D. KIRWAN · CLAY LANCASTER
MARY ELIZABETH LEACH · BURTON MILWARD · JULIA NEAL · WILLIAM RUSSELL RICE · CHARLES
GANO TALBERT · HAMBLETON TAPP · RHEA A. TAYLOR · ARNOLD WASHBURN · JOHN D. WRIGHT, JR.

TUCKY
History

J. WINSTON COLEMAN, JR., *Editor*

THOMAS D. CLARK and LAWRENCE S. THOMPSON, *Associate Editors*

CLYDE T. BURKE, *Photographic Editor*

UNIVERSITY PRESS OF KENTUCKY

WITH THE COOPERATION OF THE DEPARTMENT OF PARKS AND
THE DEPARTMENT OF PUBLIC INFORMATION OF THE COMMONWEALTH OF KENTUCKY

Lexington 1971

Picture Credits

The principal sources for illustrations used in this volume are the ten listed below. The great majority of the pictures were taken from these collections; but for others, specific credit is given.

1) Alben W. Barkley Museum, Paducah, which contains memorabilia of the Kentucky senator and vice president.

2) Berea College, the Hutchins Library and the Appalachian Museum, particularly for the photographs by Doris Ulmann.

3) Filson Club, Louisville, and its extensive library and museum of Kentuckiana.

4) Kentucky Historical Society, Frankfort, which also has a wide collection of Kentucky materials.

5) Kentucky state offices, especially the Department of Highways and that of Public Information.

6) Murray State University Library, Special Collection Division, which contains the Jesse Stuart collection.

7) University of Kentucky Library, Special Collections, with photographs from the early history of the University as well as material on Kentucky and the Ohio Valley.

8) University of Louisville, in particular the Photographic Archives on the history of Louisville and early Kentucky photographers.

9) Western Kentucky University, Bowling Green, the Kentucky Library and Museum, especially for material on the South Union Shakers.

10) Utilized also have been the personal collections of the editors.

Symbols are: (T) top, (C) center, (B) bottom, (L) left, (R) right. Figures indicate page numbers.

Albert B. Chandler Medical Center, 156; Allegheny College, 51 (TL); Roger W. Barbour, 253 (B), 254; *Blood Horse*, 224 (B); John B. Boles, 54 (TL), 55 (B); John Y. Brown, Sr., 216 (B); Brown-Forman Distillers Corp., 197 (B), 201 (T), 221 (B); Mrs. Waller O. Bullock Estates, 147 (B), 157 (T); Castleton Farm, 229 (C); Caufield & Shook, Inc., 226 (B), 227; Centre College, 216 (T); Clinton (Tenn.) Post Office, 24 (B-photo by Wilson Woolly); Henry H. Craig, Sr., 151 (B), 239 (T); E. N. Fergus, 101 (TL,B); Foster Hall Collection, 239 (B); Henry Harned, 46 (B); Danny Hatcher, 210 (BR); Michael Heatherman, 211 (T); Henry Clay Memorial Foundation, 85 (L), 86 (T); Hillerich & Bradsby, 109 (B), 212; *Horseman & Fair World*, 229 (T), 231 (B); Hunt-Morgan Home, 79 (TR); William H. Hurt, 207 (B); Willard R. Jillson, 149 (R); Thomas Joyes, 77 (top first two from left); Henry Kauffman, 25 (T); Keeneland Association, 228 (T-photo by Tony Leonard; B-photo by John C. Wyatt); Susan Jackson Keig, 159 (R-photo by James L. Ballard); Ky. Commission on Human Rights, 190 (B), 191 (B), 209 (TC); Ky. Fair & Exposition Center, 230 (T); Kentucky State College, 132 (B); Harry LaViers, 107 (B), 114 (T-photo by Charles H. Longley), 114 (B), 117 (T-photo by Charles H. Longley), 121 (T), 181 (T-photo by Charles H. Longley); Mary James Leach, 170-71; Rebecca Lee and Frances Swinford, 63 (T); *Lexington Herald-Leader*, 46 (T), 214 (BR); Lexington Public Library, 221 (T); Library of Congress, 51 (TR), 88 (TL), 89, 90; A. Z. Looney, 60 (B); *Louisville Courier-Journal & Times*, 49 (B), 72 (B), 93 (T), 95 (B), 102 (BL), 139 (B), 150 (TL), 186, 197 (TL), 208 (BR), 209 (BR), 210 (T), 217 (B), 234 (TR); James C. Mellon, 175 (BL), 195 (B); Boynton Merrill, 20 (TL), 201 (B); Pleasant Hill at Shakertown, 67, 68, 69 (B), 70 (T); National Distillers Products Co., 196 (T); Julia Neal, 66; Eurie Pearl Neel, 145 (B); New York Historical Society, 52 (B); Random House, Inc., 149 (L-photo by Harold Strauss); *Saturday Evening Post*, 211 (B-photo by Michael Bry); Spindletop Research, 250 (T); Stitzel-Weller Distillery, 199 (T), 200 (B); Jesse Stuart, 150 (B); Enos Swain, 216 (C); Taft Museum, 142 (T); Tennessee Valley Authority, 21 (B), 195 (T), 246 (B), 249 (BR); E. I. "Buddy" Thompson, 103 (B), 123 (third from top); Transylvania University, 136; Transylvania University Library, 219 (TL, B); U. S. Army, 251 (B-photo by SSG William C. Grant); U. S. Forest Service, 117 (C); U. S. Dept. of the Interior, Nat'l Park Ser., 108, 245 (B); U. S. Soil Conservation Service, 104 (B); Arnold Washburn, 223 (TL, B), 224 (C); Charlie Wright, 185 (L); Wyeth Laboratories, 155; Yellowstone Distillery, 199 (BL), 200 (TR).

First Edition 20,000 copies October 29, 1971
Second Edition 40,000 copies February 15, 1972

ISBN: 0-8131-0092-5 (cloth)
Library of Congress Catalog Card Number: 74-160043

DESIGNED BY CHARLES SKAGGS / TEXT BY ANN LEMERT

Contents

Foreword

Between the pinch of mountain range and river valleys, the land of Kentucky forms a strange lump of geography, which defies geometrical description. From the narrows of the rocky Big Sandy Gorge to the dangling penultimate island which nestles against the shoulders of Tennessee and Missouri on the Mississippi River, it is indeed a land of contrasts. That its human history should be so varied and erratic is not surprising. The long valleys which slice its eastern Appalachian face and those deep channels cut through depthless limestone domes by rivers which have ground away at the rock for centuries on end—all have witnessed processions of human beings. One may stand on the banks of Station Camp Creek, the Salt, the Bayou de Chien, Kinniconick, Barren, and Nolin and conjure up visions of American pioneers forcing their way through the wilderness to build cabins and plant new beachheads of civilization.

Long before an Anglo-American hunter penetrated the eastern mountain and river passes into Kentucky, there were prehistoric men who called the land their home. These peoples left their bodies, pottery, weapons, and utensils to be puzzled over and studied by archaeologists and anthropologists of the future, and to become the prized possessions of collectors.

The opening of Kentucky to settlement in the latter half of the eighteenth century was one of the truly dramatic incidents of American pioneering. It was not a civilization of originality that the first arrival this side of the mountains planted along the western watershed so much as it was the adaptation of an older one to a new environment, a rugged topography, and raw nature. There were few areas along the American frontier where men studded the landscape with so many visible landmarks of local interest as in Kentucky. All across the state these landmarks remain either in fact or in memory as monuments to the act of settlement.

Just as the prehistoric people documented their presence with burial sites and artifacts, the pioneers left behind abundant evidence of their existence. They left a rich legacy of primitive tools, weapons, utensils, instruments, and examples of their handicrafts. No greater contribution was made to early Kentucky than that of the early craftsmen who fashioned practical implements and some really elegant pieces of furniture from the virgin woods which they found growing on the spots where they built their cabins. These were the creations of a way of life, which now reveal what it was like to live in another time.

No act of pioneering drama took place without cost to human beings. There were the fierce pioneers who resisted Indian raids, those who struggled with the elements and the land, and those who laid foundations for human institutions. All of these have been fused into an image of men garbed in homespun and crude leather, weather-burned and calloused, experts with ox, plow, gun, and froe, inured to hardships, and predestinarian in philosophy. These were the faceless ones who patiently cleared openings in the forest, built homes and towns, and who grazed animals and produced farm products for new western markets. These were the ones who trampled primitive forest trails into highways, furrowed the soil, and in time rode pitching flatboats down the great rivers in search of merchants and cash for the products of field, smokehouse, and still.

Kentucky, however, had plenty of faces among its pioneers, of individuals whose names personified much of the broader westward movement, even well beyond the borders of the state. In an ever-shifting human drama, buckskinned woodsmen now turned Kentuckians; prosperous farmers, local and national politicians, doctors, professors, preachers, artists, authors, newspaper editors, soldiers, and scientists were to exert far-flung influence. It was they who in time gave Kentucky history its profound personal quality.

Political foundations and expansion in the eighteenth and nineteenth centuries involved both men and events in movements which stirred the whole national scene. Kentuckians formed a state after debating and compromising controversial political theories and issues. They fought in regional and national wars, they helped to compromise explosive national issues and to create others, they sat in legislative halls and in Congress, at peace tables, and served at foreign courts as diplomats. They rushed ahead with the spreading American frontiers to the West and South to help form new states, to sit in governors' chairs, to preside as judges, and to lift voices in legislative oratory. Ever, the Kentuckian has been a political animal. He has adorned his public halls and his archival and art collections with graphic evidence of this fact in the forms of busts, portraits, commissions, and political memorabilia.

In a more refined vein the settlers brought in their saddlebags the germs of institutional culture. They raised churches and schools, and established libraries, special interest societies, towns, and communities on the face of the land. These they nurtured from one generation to the next. From the old Mulkey Meeting House in Monroe County to the sophisticated Speed Museum of Art in Louisville, cultural landmarks in the state are plentiful. Also, the monuments to recurring eras of economic growth reflect the impact of the farmer, the merchant, miner, industrialist, and the artisan.

Hardly had the first settler leaned his broadaxe against a tree before the age of economic change was upon Kentucky. Racing headlong into the future, communities have flourished or perished as they were favored or spurned by the constant process of economic revolution in America. In both eastern and western Kentucky miners have tunneled the bowels of the earth to gather millions of tons of precious coal; in an even more ravenous mood they have scarred the land with their behemoth strip-mining machines. They have mauled and destroyed blocks of forests, choked streams, and left evidence of their avarice that future generations will shudder at. Industrial sites have been developed all over the state. There are those also which mark the existence of industries no longer in existence. Old iron furnaces, for instance, tell stories of another age and another dream of prosperity.

Once-fine country homes have disappeared or are slowly melting into the landscape from neglect and decay. This reflects not only a changing pattern of the agrarian way of life in Kentucky, but also a well-nigh complete shift in the nature of family organization and attitudes. What once was a strongly centralized patriarchial, family-based society has now lost ground to a more detached urban way of life. The older homes are still cherished, but the new pattern is ring after ring of town and suburban houses which within themselves document the rapidly changing nature of human organization in Kentucky.

The landscape of Kentucky has become striped in recent years with double ribbons of super high-speed roads. In many instances these all but obliterate the old trails over which pioneers struggled westward with families and pack animals. Thus it is that the history of Kentucky has ever been one of contrast and change. It may at times have been frustrating and self-defeating in nature. At others it may have had its glorious and satisfying moments, but it has never been dull. Even the most illiterate and deprived Kentuckians have exhibited strong personal pride, expressed sometimes in forms of heedless anger and violence, but at other times in the warmest possible terms of humanity and dignity. The variety often is too great and too complex for the historian to capture in word and phrase, or even to document from trusted and objective sources.

The camera can be more discerning as to detail. So can the cartographer and geographer. They can locate and portray with dependable precision the finer distinctions of the rich and exciting contrasts.

If the human side of Kentucky presents contrasts of spiritual subleties, the face of the land offers an even greater variety of beauty and nostalgic appeal. Caught in the focus of the photographer's lens or on an artist's canvas, it stands revealed in its power, its starkness, sometimes in ugliness, but always in detail. Contained in this volume are the portraits of landmarks, men, and events which have related Kentuckians to their land and the times. It portrays the degree in which they have cooperated with their environment, and in which they have spurned it. This volume is wide ranging in scope of space and time, institutional growth, in humanity, and, most of all, in portraying the changes of a dynamic society. In its simple clarity, it graphically documents the advances Kentuckians have made on the wider scale of American civilization and the degree to which they have retained their regional individuality.

Thomas D. Clark
June 12, 1971

I. PREHISTORY

Modern archeological research has shown that the prehistoric people of the New World were the direct ancestors of the American Indian and that they came into North America from Asia by way of the Bering Straits more than 16,000 years ago.

Cultural changes following the arrival of these people are distinctive enough that archeologists have divided Kentucky's prehistory into six cultures. These are: the Paleo-Indian from 13,000 to 6000 B.C.; the Archaic from 6000 to 1000 B.C.; the Woodland from 1000 B.C. to 900 A.D.; the Adena from 800 B.C. to 800 A.D.; the Mississippian in western Kentucky from 1000 to 1600 A.D.; and the Fort Ancient in the Bluegrass and eastern mountains from 1200 to 1650 A.D.

The early part of the Paleo-Indian period, during the last Ice Age, saw the migration from Asia across the Bering Straits into North America. The Paleo-Indians were nomadic hunters who lived by preying upon large mammals, which they killed with a spear, tipped with a distinctive, fluted stone point.

Archaic people lived a semisedentary life, moving about during part of the year and settling at other times along river banks. There they gathered mussels and plant foods, fished, and hunted game with the spear and spearthrower. Apparently these people had no knowledge of agriculture or pottery making. Their dead were buried in round pits with the bodies flexed, and sometimes tools were included in the burial.

In the Woodland period hunting, fishing, and food gathering were supplemented by agriculture. These people cultivated sunflowers, marsh elder, giant ragweed, and squash. They continued to use the spear and spearthrower in hunting, but during the latter part of this period also began to use the bow and arrow.

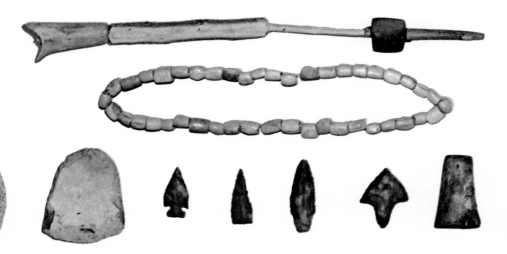

8

The Adena Culture developed from a Woodland base. Adena people became more dependent on cultivating Woodland crops while continuing to hunt and to gather other plant foods. They lived in circular houses with conical roofs and slightly outsloping walls grouped in small, scattered villages. They made pottery and fashioned various ornaments of mica and copper. They continued to use the spear and spearthrower and the bow and arrow in hunting game. The Adena cremated many of their dead, although a few were buried in log tombs covered with earth mounds.

The Mississippian Culture saw an increased population occupying large stockaded villages that included flat-topped temple mounds. They lived in mud-walled, thatched houses. Agriculture was almost entirely confined to river bottom land, and the principal crops were corn, beans, and squash. The Mississippian people hunted with the bow and arrow, made pottery with effigy forms, and fashioned large chipped stone knives, celts, picks, and hoes.

Fort Ancient Culture was a continuation of Woodland with influences from the Mississippian. The people lived in rectangular or oval houses grouped in small villages. Their diet was corn, beans, and squash supplemented with fish and wild game, which they hunted primarily with the bow and arrow. They used pottery for food and water, and they carved shell gorgets incised with human faces. During late Fort Ancient times some European trade goods began to appear among the native artifacts.

Indian tribes found in Kentucky just prior to the coming of the pioneers were the Shawnee, Cherokee, and Chickasaw.

II. PIONEER ERA

When the first white explorers reached Kentucky—the legendary "Dark and Bloody Ground" or "Great Meadow"—they found few Indians living there despite the region's abundant game and other natural resources. The fabled hunting ground was, instead, visited and fought over by tribes who lived north of the Ohio and south of the Cumberland.

Although Virginia claimed title to the western lands under her royal charter of 1609, she was not hasty to explore the transmontane regions. But by 1729 or earlier, travelers and hunters had visited Big Bone Lick. In 1750 Dr. Thomas Walker came close to the central Bluegrass area, and Christopher Gist passed through Kentucky while exploring for the Ohio Land Company in 1751. Hunters' stories of bountiful game and fertile land, often exaggerated, whetted the appetites of land-hungry eastern settlers.

When the French relinquished their claims to the western territories in 1763, a royal decree set those lands aside for the loyal Indian subjects of the English king. American colonists, however, acquiring the land by treaties and purchases, extinguished the claims, but not the hostility, of the Indians.

Daniel Boone first entered Kentucky in 1767 and explored as far as the Kentucky and Red River valleys in 1769. In 1771 Simon Kenton went into northern Kentucky. Amidst the rush for new

land George Washington drove one of the first claim stakes, on the Big Sandy in 1770.

Following the scouts, settlers began to cross the Alleghenies despite Indian harassment and the harsh conditions of frontier life. The first permanent white settlement was established by James Harrod in 1774 near the present city of Harrodsburg. The year before, Boone attempted to bring his and several other families into Kentucky, but was turned back by an Indian attack. His Boonesborough settlement in 1775 was more fortunate. Here is Boone's story, according to John Filson's 1784 historical sketch of Kentucky:

> I foon began this work, having collected a number of enterprifing men, well armed   We proceeded with all poffible expedition until we came within fifteen miles of where Boonfborough now ftands, and where we were fired upon by a party of Indians that killed two, and wounded two of our number; yet, although furprifed and taken at a difadvantage, we ftood our ground. This was on the twentieth of March, 1775. Three days after, we were fired upon again, and had two men killed, and three wounded. Afterwards we proceeded on to Kentucke river without oppofition; and on the firft day of April began to erect the fort of Boonfborough at a falt lick, about fixty yards from the river, on the S. fide.

From these first settlers sprang a vigorous new society in the wilderness, the vanguard of a restless, ever-westward movement to the Pacific.

A buckskin hunting shirt, said to have belonged to Daniel Boone, at the Filson Club, Louisville.

A pioneer western hunter (above), from Collins's *Historical Sketches of Kentucky.*

The Indian and Explorer Trails of Kentucky

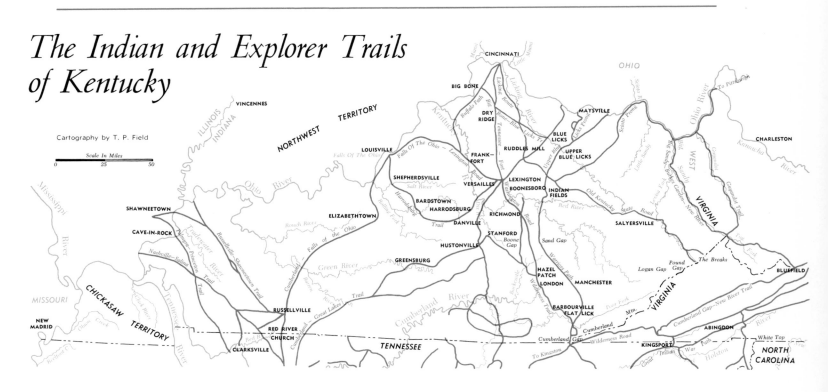

Cartography by T. P. Field

The early explorers used well-traveled Indian routes before the building of regular roads. Some of these trails are followed by present-day highways: the Wilderness Trail is basically U.S. 25; the Old Kentucky State Road is the Mountain Parkway; Interstate 65 follows the Cumberland–Falls of the Ohio route.

Indian-fighter Simon Kenton, whose exploits and survival ability equaled those of Daniel Boone, was captured by Indians in 1778. The savages stripped him, cruelly tied him on the back of a horse, and sent him on a wild ride through the forest as shown in the romantic painting above.

Dagnieau De Quindre, a French-Canadian militia-man leading 400 Indians, tried in 1778 to trick Boonesborough's defenders by negotiating a treaty outside the fort (above). The ruse failed and the settlers regained the safety of the stockade. Raise of the ensuing siege saved other Kentucky forts.

Fort Boonesborough, which is seen in an artist's rendering above, was protected by the Kentucky River as well as furnished with a ready supply of fresh water, important features in case of attack.

John Filson's *Discovery, Settlement and Present State of Kentucke,* published in 1784, was the first book on the Commonwealth. It is more a traveler's guide than a history. Perhaps its most popular feature was an appendix, "The Adventures of Col. Daniel Boon," which is said to have so delighted Boone that he declared every word of it true. The map, issued with the book and published separately many times, was quite good for its day. Filson arrived in the West in 1783 and opened a private school in Lexington. His portrait, at right, is by A. O. Revenaugh.

The Development of Kentucky Counties

After John Filson's *A Map of Kentucky* (1784)

Cartography by T. P. Field

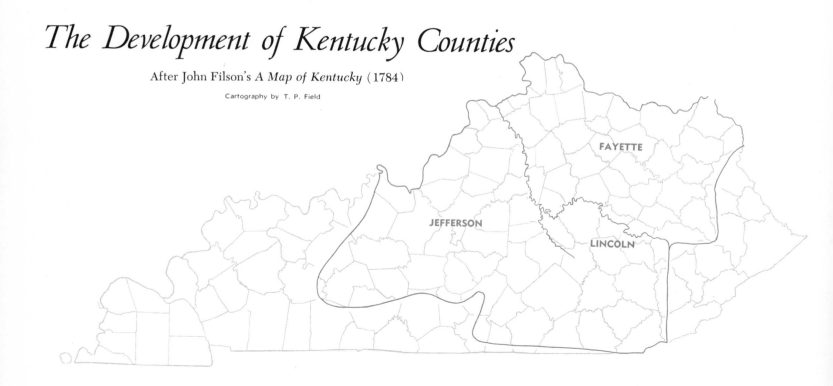

Immediately above, Aaron Reynolds helps Captain Robert Patterson escape at the Battle of Blue Licks (August 19, 1782), giving up his own horse. He was rewarded with 200 acres of good land.

The wood engraving (top of page) depicts the capture of two daughters of Colonel Richard Calloway and Daniel Boone's daughter Jemima, within sight of Boonesborough on July 7, 1776.

(Above) Boone and his party, after tracking the Indian captors of the three girls all night, saved the girls the next day without harm to them or their rescuers.

Mrs. John Merril (right) defended her wounded husband in a midnight Indian attack on their Nelson County cabin. Besides using an ax effectively, she threw feather pillows into the fireplace and smoked out several other Indians.

Virginia's law of primogeniture, under which the eldest son inherited all of the father's proper-ty, encouraged many of the younger sons of wealthy families (above) to migrate to Kentucky.

The Development of Kentucky Counties

After J. Russell's *Map of the State of Kentucky with Adjoining Territories* (1794)

Cartography by T. P. Field

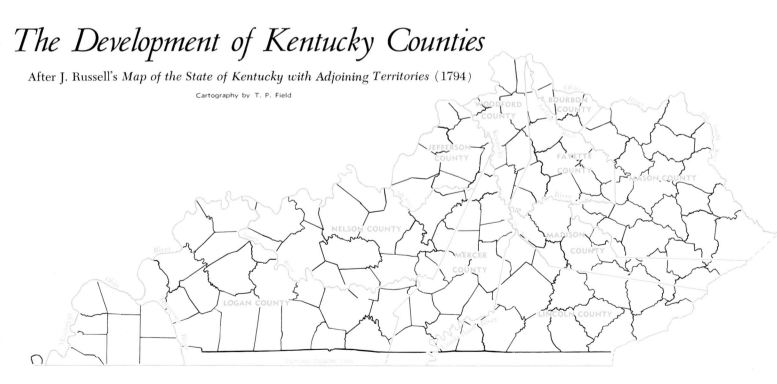

Russell's map is generally more informative than Filson's. Except for several river boundaries, however, nearly all of his indicated county lines have subsequently been altered.

These reconstructions of pioneer buildings include a replica of Abraham Lincoln's boyhood home (above) on Knob Creek. As an adult, Lincoln referred to his family's Knob Creek homestead as the first place he could recall. McHargue's Mill (above right) stands in Levi Jackson Wilderness Road State Park at London. Built in 1812, it was reconstructed in 1938. At right is the Dr. Thomas Walker State Shrine, a reproduction of the cabin built by the explorer-doctor in 1750. The original was one of the first non-Indian dwellings erected in Kentucky.

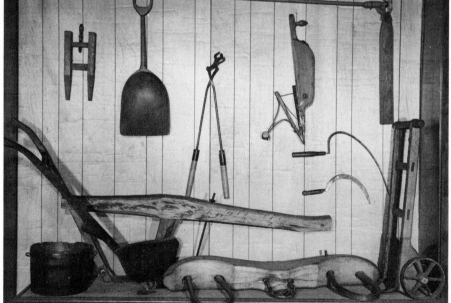

Dolls like these once delighted the hearts of little pioneer girls (left to right): pen wiper doll, dried apple doll, leather Indian doll, two corn shuck dolls, and a hickory nut doll.

At left are farm tools and fireplace implements of the period.

Frontier hero Simon Kenton, a forgotten man in his old age, had to petition the state, which he had served so well, for a small yearly pension.

Richard Henderson, whose Transylvania Company was instrumental in establishing Fort Boonesborough, dreamed of carving out an empire in the West.

The Development of Kentucky Counties

After Luke Munsell's *A Map of the State of Kentucky* (1818)

Cartography by T. P. Field

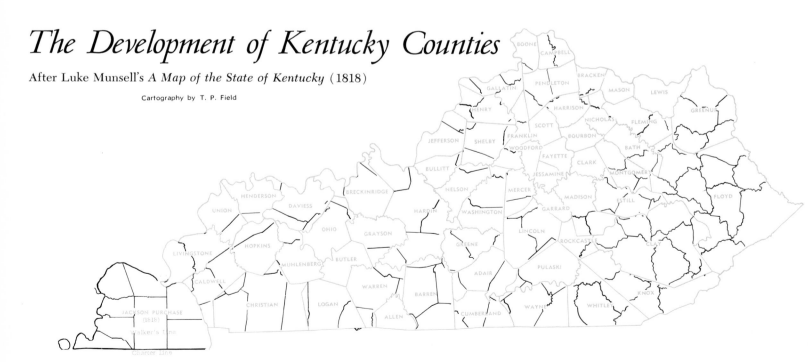

At the time of Munsell's official state map the southern boundary was surveyed and, with few exceptions, fixed. The meridians, however, were still over twenty miles west of their true positions. Only ten counties had their permanent boundaries.

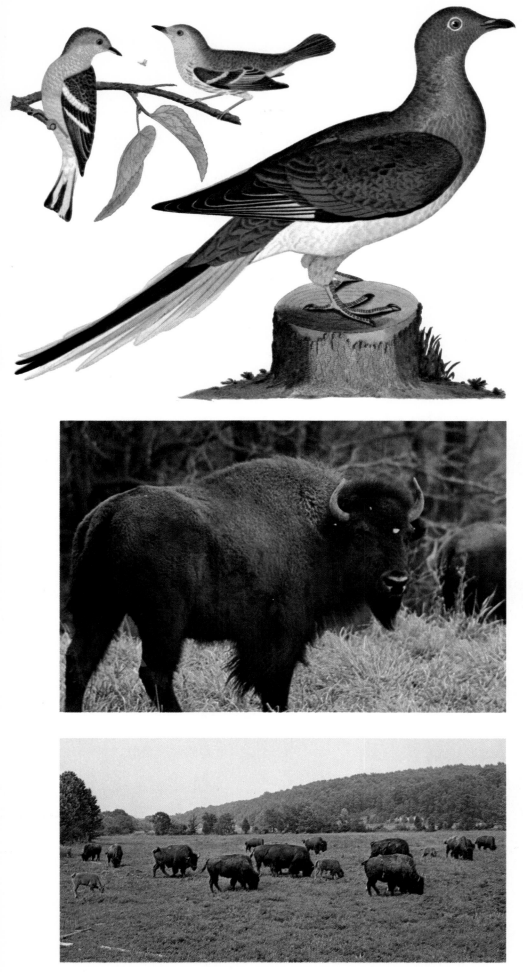

In the tales of hunters and traders Kentucky emerged as a new Eden. And in fact it did possess magnificent virgin forests, grassy savannas and canebrakes, numerous streams and salt licks. The Indians who hunted across Kentucky kept the grasslands open and free of brush by burning them each year. On this lush pasturage fattened herds of deer, buffalo, and elk. Other wildlife was equally plentiful.

In spite of their numbers, some species were doomed to extinction by reckless hunting practices and by the use of land for agriculture. Buffalo, hunted extensively during the great westward movement, are now found only in herds such as this one grazing in the Land Between the Lakes, a recreation and conservation education area in western Kentucky. Less fortunate, the passenger pigeon (top left), which once darkened the skies with its huge flocks, finally succumbed to the white man's relentless slaughter.

A replica of the Lincoln homestead (immediately below) stands five miles north of Springfield, Washington County. The area where the president's grandfather grew to manhood now comprises a state park, which is a repository of fascinating Lincoln lore. The monument at right marks the grave of Daniel Boone. It stands in the Frankfort Cemetery on a bluff overlooking the Kentucky River.

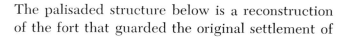

The palisaded structure below is a reconstruction of the fort that guarded the original settlement of Harrodsburg. It now forms a part of Old Fort Harrod State Park.

III. REVOLUTION AND STATEHOOD

WHEN news of Lexington and Concord reached the West in 1775, the fledgling settlements correctly expected the British to incite Indian attacks against them. By 1777 intensive Indian raids drove all the western settlers into four forts: Harrod's, Boone's, Logan's, and McClelland's.

To relieve the Kentuckians, George Rogers Clark took the British forts at Kaskaskia and Cahokia on the Mississippi. By capturing Vincennes in 1779, he broke British control in the West for a time. Daniel Boone's daring escape from Indian capture in 1778 enabled him to warn and save other Bluegrass forts.

The final battle of the Revolutionary War, the Battle of Blue Licks, was fought in Kentucky in 1782. Although a disaster for the Americans, it was the last major engagement with Indians in Kentucky. With the war's end in 1783 only small raiding parties continued to molest settlers, and no longer were they guided by British leaders. Kentuckians had succeeded in defending the West for the new United States, although statehood for Kentucky was not achieved until 1792.

Even during the Revolutionary War the population of Kentucky grew and by 1783 had reached 12,000. In 1790 the first national census recorded 73,677 inhabitants.

Simultaneously demands increased to separate from the remote government in Virginia. A conference in Danville in 1784 became the first in a series of ten meetings leading to statehood. Finally, after disappointing delays and dissension, Kentucky became the fifteenth state on June 1, 1792, the first west of the Alleghenies.

Signatures of men prominent in Kentucky's early history: Dr. Thomas Walker, Daniel Boone, Simon Kenton, George Rogers Clark, Christopher Gist, George Washington, Patrick Henry (governor of Virginia when Kentucky was formally established as a county of that state), and Alexander D. Orr (one of Kentucky's first two representatives in the United States Congress).

Kentucky's Indian problem did not vanish with statehood. The settlements were threatened by British-Indian alliances north of the Ohio until England's hold on the Northwest was broken at the Battle of the Thames in 1813, where Tecumseh was killed (above). Kentuckians played a prominent role in the battle.

By the Jackson Purchase of 1818, the Chickasaws gave up the rest of their lands in Kentucky and Tennessee. In the mural at right, Isaac Shelby, Kentucky's first governor, and General Andrew Jackson prepare to sign the treaty with representative chiefs of the Chickasaw Nation.

Isaac Shelby (below), hero of the Battle of King's Mountain during the Revolutionary War, was Kentucky's first governor. He took the oath of office at Lexington, the Commonwealth's first seat of government, June 4, 1792. In 1812 he was reelected to a second term, supporting the popular demand for war with England over the Northwest Territory. The old soldier, progenitor of a famous Kentucky family, took personal command of 4000 Kentucky volunteers and joined General William Henry Harrison in the invasion of Canada, which led to the British defeat at the Battle of the Thames in 1813.

The turmoil of Kentucky's early years was heightened by several conspiracies, the first of which was James Wilkinson's scheme that was followed by a French conspiracy in 1793. And in 1805 Aaron Burr appeared in Kentucky amid rumors of plans to create an independent republic.

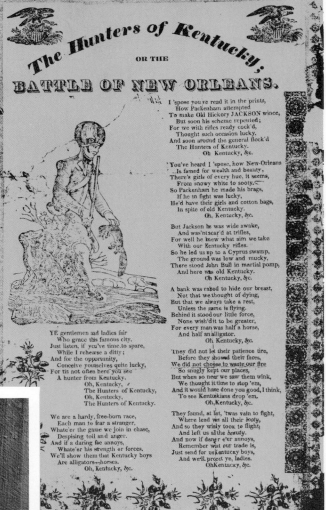

The warrior image cherished by the frontiersman—"half horse, half alligator"—was extolled in the ballad above celebrating the surprising American victory at the Battle of New Orleans in 1815.

By the end of the Revolution, however, men of more wealth and education were migrating to Kentucky, where these new aristocrats quickly assumed political, social, and economic leadership.

25

IV. ANTEBELLUM PERIOD

THE CRUDENESS of frontier life in the new West was beginning to diminish in the early nineteenth century. By this time, although still provincial and agrarian, Kentucky's society had acquired some of the polish and urbanity of the East. Towns such as Lexington, Bardstown, and Danville could boast of imposing homes, schools and academies, racetracks, and a small but versatile intelligentsia.

From 1797, newspapers, books, and periodicals became increasingly available. New ideas in science, religion, education, literature, and the arts flowed into and made their mark upon Kentucky. The national contest between the Federalists and the Jeffersonians stirred partisans here too, as witnessed by the stormy career of Humphrey Marshall (above left), whose staunch devotion to the principle of a strong central government embroiled him with other Kentuckians, nearly all of whom favored an individualistic democracy.

Kentuckians by the 1840s were again ready to fight to secure interests they considered vital. With the British safely out of the Northwest, their attention turned toward Texas and the boundary dispute with Mexico.

Mexican War

When General Zachary Taylor (left) invaded Texas in 1846, most Kentuckians favored the resulting war with Mexico. The profitable extension of cotton farming and slavery to the vast southwestern territory had already enticed many of them to settle there.

Because of the many Kentuckians among the 50,000 American settlers in Texas by 1844 the annexation of Texas became a vital issue not only in the new territory but back home as well. When Texans fought for independence from Mexico, Kentuckians led some divisions of the rebel army. When the United States entered the conflict in 1846, the Commonwealth was well represented in the ranks of volunteers. At left is the regimental flag of the Second Regiment, Kentucky Volunteers.

The Battle of Buena Vista in February 1847—a hard-fought, drawn battle followed by a Mexican retreat—resulted in many Kentucky casualties, among them Lieutenant Colonel Henry Clay, Jr. (above), of the Second Regiment. The young officer's death was a second war-connected tragedy for the senior Clay, who lost the 1844 presidential election because he had opposed war with Mexico.

The Treaty of Guadalupe Hidalgo, signed in 1848, resolved the boundary dispute in the Southwest which had concerned Kentuckians for years. So popular was the war in the Commonwealth that politicians traded successfully upon even slight associations with Taylor and Buena Vista. The monument in the Frankfort Cemetery (below) was erected by the Commonwealth to honor all soldiers from the Mexican War to the present.

Known fondly to his troops by the colorful nickname of "Old Rough and Ready," General Taylor achieved political fortune from his victory at Buena Vista and the annexation of Texas. His popularity as a military hero gained him the Whig nomination for the presidency in 1848, and he won a narrow victory over Lewis Cass of Michigan in an election prophetic of the bitter division over slavery that was to come. He became the first Kentuckian to enter the White House, but his term of office, cut short by a fatal illness, lasted only sixteen months. Taylor's battles, from the War of 1812 to his victories in Mexico, are depicted on the broadside above. Born in Virginia, Taylor spent his early years in Kentucky where as a young man he assisted in management of his father's estate. His burial place is now a national cemetery northeast of Louisville. Nearby stands the family home Springfield.

Homes

As FRONTIER conditions became more secure, the settlers' crude and hastily-built log shelters were replaced by more permanent homes. Henry Clay's Ashland (below) reflected Lexington's early prominence as a cultural center. Noted architect Benjamin Latrobe designed the wings for the original house, the main part of which was built earlier. Torn down in 1856, Ashland was rebuilt along the same general lines in 1857.

The elegant parlor of Ashland (above), with its rare gold dust mirror and French gold brocade draperies, clearly indicates the wealth and taste that were present in Kentucky. Built in 1805-1806, the original Ashland was a far cry from the settler's simple, utilitarian cabin with its sparse furnishings, its walls chinked with mud and stones, and its dirt or puncheon floor.

Even while Indian raids threatened, however, some impressive early homes were built. Some of these were houses planned with attention both to the niceties of polite society and to frontier realities: more than one large home possessed not only a ballroom but a secret chamber to enable the family to escape from marauding savages.

Early in the nineteenth century the danger from Indians ended. As Kentuckians recovered from the economic reverses following the War of 1812, the demand for home building increased. In this safer, more affluent period people grew eager to display their new wealth in more imposing homes, richer furnishings, and tastefully laid out grounds.

From an early date there were skilled architects and builders in Kentucky, men such as John McMurtry, Thomas Lewinski, Mathias Shryock, and his sons Gideon and Cincinnatus. Architects from outside the state, among them Thomas Jefferson, also designed homes in the Commonwealth.

Lexington architect Gideon Shryock (left), introduced the impressive Greek Revival style to Kentucky when he built the Old State House in Frankfort in 1827-1830. Constructed of white limestone quarried from the Kentucky River bluffs, it is dominated by a severely plain Ionic portico supported by columns four feet in diameter and thirty-three feet high. Its imposing proportions and balance proved irresistible to the classical-minded Kentucky aristocracy. After 1830 many homes designed for well-to-do planters were done in the Greek Revival style.

The Old Governor's Mansion in Frankfort (below) has served as home for Kentucky's lieutenant governors since its renovation in 1956. From 1797 until 1914 it was the official residence of thirty-three governors. One of them, Thomas "Stone Hammer" Metcalfe, laid the stone foundation, returning later as the state's tenth governor.

Home of Governor Isaac Shelby, Traveller's Rest was built in 1786 in Lincoln County and is said to have been the first stone house in the state. The house, later destroyed by fire, is shown as it appeared on an old postcard (right). A monument to Shelby stands in the nearby family burial ground.

As prosperous settlers from North Carolina, Virginia, Maryland, and Pennsylvania moved west, they tended to build homes much like the ones they had left. A good example of Dominion Georgian architecture in Kentucky is Liberty Hall (right), built in 1796 by John Brown of Virginia. Brown was the first congressman from the District of Kentucky (at that time still part of Virginia) and later the first United States senator from the state of Kentucky.

Now maintained as a shrine by the Kentucky chapter of the National Society of the Colonial Dames of America, the brick house was once an important political and social gathering place. James Monroe, Lafayette, William Henry Harrison, Andrew Jackson, Zachary Taylor, and Theodore Roosevelt are among the notables who have been entertained here.

The Georgian house in Lexington (above) was the girlhood home of Mary Todd. Although Abraham Lincoln is generally thought to have courted Mary here, they first met when she visited a sister in Springfield, Illinois. Married in Springfield, the Lincolns later returned for visits here.

George Rogers Clark spent his last days at Locust Grove (below), built around 1800 near Louisville by his brother-in-law. This house, a handsome example of the Kentucky version of Georgian architecture, has been restored as one of the state's most historic shrines.

Farmington, designed by Thomas Jefferson and built in 1810 near Louisville, contains a reminder of frontier dangers. A secret stairway, hidden between the main hall and ground floor, provided a way of escape in case of Indian attack. James Speed, a son of the builder, and attorney-general in Abraham Lincoln's cabinet, was at the President's bedside when he died. The deed to the property, dated 1780, was signed by Patrick Henry.

Captain Thomas Marshall, Jr., brother of Chief Justice John Marshall, constructed this Georgian house (below) about 1800 in Washington, Mason County. Brick for the house was burned on the place.

Pleasant Lawn (above), a distinctive home near Versailles in Woodford County, was designed by a pioneer landowner who knew what he wanted in a house and incorporated his own ideas in the plans. The central part has ceilings that are fourteen feet high. Arches connect the round brick pillars (left) across the recessed front porch. Painted on the plastered walls of the large parlor are murals portraying scenes from the state's early history. Pleasant Lawn was built in 1829.

Glengarry, or Cane Run (above), was an Italianate villa built in 1854 three miles north of Lexington for a wealthy hemp dealer. Major Thomas Lew- inski designed Glengarry and its three-story tower. It was considered to be one of the finest examples of its type in America.

Near his Sportsman's Hill (right) in Lincoln County, Colonel William Whitley laid out a "race path" while finishing his fine home, 1787-1790. From the hill spectators could have a good view of the horses running below. Indian-fighter and legislator, Whitley included a hiding place from Indians in the third-floor ballroom. He met his death during the Battle of the Thames in 1813, and his handsome home is now a state shrine. It is thought to be the first brick house built in Kentucky.

Twin ice houses (above) at Ashland cooled the milk, butter, and other perishable foods for the large domestic establishment of Henry Clay. Such a refinement enabled Mrs. Clay to enjoy her favorite ice cream and to serve cool drinks despite the heat of a Kentucky summer.

The sturdy two-story log house (left), near West Liberty in Morgan County, has been standing since about 1850. It resembles the first homes built by the settlers after the danger from Indian attacks had subsided and they could move out of the stockades onto their new land. Since there were no sawmills at that time, the timbers for these simple homes were shaped with an adz. Many log houses were later covered with weatherboarding as lumber became available.

37

Four towers distinguished the Gothic Revival Ingelside (above), which for over a century stood near Lexington, a medieval "castle" in the Bluegrass. The cloverleaf design above the front entrance is characteristic of the architect John McMurtry, who had traveled in England and France to study their architecture before designing Ingelside. Another Gothic castle, Loudoun, was built near Lexington by Francis Key Hunt, a wealthy landowner, during the same period, 1850-1852. It is now used by the Lexington Department of Recreation.

The clapboard house (above) in Washington, Mason County, was the home of Doctor John Johnston, who moved to Kentucky in 1788 and for years was the only physician in the area. His youngest son, General Albert Sidney Johnston, was Confederate commander in the West when he was killed in the Battle of Shiloh in 1862. The house is now owned by the local chapter of the Daughters of the American Revolution.

Located in Knox County on the Wilderness Road into Kentucky, the Rasnic house had endured for about 150 years when it burned in 1945. Its construction exhibits many features of the more substantial cabins built by the settlers after their first primitive shelters—the squared logs with half-dovetail joints, the hand-split shingles or "shakes," the small lean-to added at the rear of the house, the half-attic indicated by the small window over the porch. Notable is the massive stone chimney. In earlier homes the chimney was frequently made of small logs lined with mud, which the heat baked to a pottery-like hardness.

Settlers in Kentucky's mountains often found their surroundings beautiful, and today the moun-

tain people are fiercely loyal to their land. But their lives were not easy. Steep ridges made travel difficult, and isolation was an accepted part of life. Land suitable for crops was limited, and farming was hard and unprofitable.

Frontier conditions lingered in the mountains until early in the twentieth century. Domestic architecture there accordingly represented the necessities of life. A log house with a dog-trot down the middle was cool in summer; well-chinked, with its large fireplace, it could be warm in winter. The half-attic accommodated the mountaineer's usually large family. Unfortunately few of these once sturdy reminders of the past have survived fire and the perishability of unpainted timbers.

Stately Walnut Hall (below) near Lexington in Fayette County contrasts sharply with the simple cabin at right, clearly marking the differences between the Bluegrass and the eastern mountains. Surveyed in 1777 by a Revolutionary War veteran, Walnut Hall Farm is located in central Kentucky whose fertile soil meant wealth for its owners. Long a famous breeding farm for trotting horses, Walnut Hall has a cemetery in which several of its well-known horses (including Guy Axworthy) are buried. The present house was built in 1842.

Along Minnie's Niece Branch, Elliott County, in the mountains of the Cumberland Plateau.

Massive, beautifully proportioned Wickland (above), the ancestral home of the Wickliffe family in Bardstown, has been the home of three governors: Charles A. Wickliffe and J. C. Wickliffe Beckham of Kentucky and Robert C. Wickliffe of Louisiana.

In 1788, four years before Kentucky became a state, Major Joseph Duncan built the tavern (left) that bears his name, overlooking the town square of Paris in Bourbon County. The Georgian structure was originally a combination tavern and inn and was in operation for over 150 years. It is now the headquarters for the Kentucky Society of the Daughters of the American Revolution, who restored the building during the 1950s.

Both the Hunt-Morgan house (above) in Lexington and Edgewood (right) in Bardstown, built at about the same time (1812-1815), are associated with Civil War personalities and events. The Hunt-Morgan house, Hopemont, was built by John Wesley Hunt, the first millionaire west of the Alleghenies. His dashing grandson, General John Hunt Morgan, won fame as the "Thunderbolt of the Confederacy." The General's nephew, Thomas Hunt Morgan, who received the Nobel Prize for his research in genetics, was born here.

Edgewood served as headquarters for General Leonidas Polk during the Confederate occupation of Bardstown. The right wing is the older portion. Benjamin Hardin, Kentucky lawyer and secretary of state, built Edgewood. His grandson, General Ben Hardin Helm of the Confederate army, who was born at Edgewood, married Emilie Todd, sister of Mrs. Lincoln.

Of all the early nineteenth century homes in Kentucky perhaps the best known is Federal Hill. The old John Rowan home in Bardstown is traditionally considered the inspiration for the ballad "My Old Kentucky Home" by Stephen Foster, who is said to have visited his cousins here in the early 1850s.

The older part of the house, now the rear wing, was completed by John Rowan in 1795. Over twenty years later the main part, consisting of two stories and a low attic, was finished. The interior is distinguished by beautifully carved wooden mantels in each room. Like many other fine Southern homes Federal Hill has a long tradition of lavish hospitality afforded to famous guests—and in its history at least one duel.

The house remained in the Rowan family until 1922 when it was acquired by the state and made into a shrine. Now thousands of visitors annually tour its halls and grounds. To many Kentuckians and to many from outside the Commonwealth, Federal Hill and the song linked with it have become symbols of the colorful life of a bygone time whose aura lingers on today.

Slavery

As I would not be a _slave_, so I would not be a _master_. This expresses my idea of democracy.— Whatever differs from this, to the extent of the difference, is no democracy.—

A. Lincoln—

ABRAHAM LINCOLN's views on Negro slavery (top of page) were not shared by all Kentuckians. When the new state entered the Union in 1792, its constitution recognized the "peculiar institution." From the 1840s to 1861 Kentucky's surplus slaves were an important export to the southern states.

Common to all the American colonies, slavery first crossed the mountains into Kentucky as settlers from Virginia brought their human chattels along with their livestock and household goods. Master and slave fought together against their common enemy, the Indian. In 1790 slaves numbered about 12,000 of a total population of 75,000.

Kentucky's patriarchal system of slavery was traditionally the mildest in any of the southern states. Its unhappy aspects, however, are illustrated in the newspaper advertisement of a slave trader of the 1850s (below, left) and in the old engraving (below) which shows slaves "sold down the river" being loaded on a Mississippi steamboat for shipment to southern slave markets.

A LARGE NUMBER
OF
NEGROES
WANTED!
The undersigned wishes to purchase throughout the year, a large number of
SOUND AND HEALTH
Negroes
OF BOTH SEXES.

FOR which the HIGHEST PRICE IN CASH will be paid at his Jail, opposite the County Jail, Short Street, Lexington, Ky., where either himself or his Agents L. C. & A. O. Robards, at all times may be found.

Any letters addressed to me concerning negroes, shall have prompt attention.

Dec. 16-25 6mo.   R. W. LUCAS.

I Robert S. Todd of the City of Lexington do hereby make & ordain this my last will & testament, I give to my wife Elizabeth Todd thirty acres of land situated in Franklin, also her two slaves sam field & Harvey also Chaney & her two children Jim, Mary during her natural life then to descend to the children heirs at law — The balance of my estate after winding up the affairs of Oldham Todd & Co & other concerns I wish divided equally in just proportions between my first & second children — I appoint David Humphreys, Dana Breck & William Rhodes executors of my estate, giving them full power to act in every capacity and every way as well in their opinion, further the interests of my estate — also to my wife Elizabeth Todd my carriage horses & household furniture

R. S. Todd

I direct that wm be sold

In Kentucky, slavery was more of a domestic than a commercial institution, for agricultural conditions and climate were not suited to the profitable year-round use of slave labor.

Robert S. Todd's will (above) gave his property, including slaves, to his heirs—among them his daughter Mary Todd Lincoln, wife of the President. On this basis, Lincoln's political enemies later charged that he had been a slave owner.

Many slaves fled to Canada and to "free" states north of the Ohio. The advertisement for a missing slave (below, right) offers a greater reward if the runaway was captured in another state, for often the return of a slave from a free state was difficult. A typical log slave cabin is shown below.

Slaves were often freed by their masters; others managed to buy their freedom. The Kentucky Colonization Society transported freed slaves to a colony in Liberia but the project ended in failure after thirty years, having sent only about twenty-two Negroes a year to Africa.

Lincoln's Emancipation Proclamation of 1863 did not apply to Kentucky and other states which did not secede, but practically it spelled the end of slavery. Passage of the Thirteenth Amendment to the Constitution in 1865 legally abolished the system of human bondage which had existed in Kentucky for well over three-quarters of a century.

$200 REWARD.
RUNAWAY

FROM the subscriber, living at White Sulphur, Scott county, Ky., a Negro Man named CHARLES. He is about 5 feet 11 inches high, or 6 feet high, about 19 years of age, of black complexion, weighs about 180 pounds, and holds his head one sided. He is a very likely man. He had on when he left a brown coat and striped pants.

I will give a reward of $100 if taken any where in this State, or $200 if taken out of the State, and delivered at Lewis C. Robards' jail, in Lexington, Ky., or secured in jail so I get him; and in either case all reasonable expenses will be paid. SANFORD DAVIS.

Scott county, July 22, 1853—85-4t

The windowless, two-story brick and stone portion of the building at right was the Fayette County Jail in Lexington, where captured runaway slaves were housed until they were claimed by their owners. The left side was the jailor's residence.

Harriet Beecher Stowe gathered material for *Uncle Tom's Cabin* while visiting the Thomas Kennedy house in Garrard County (right) and the Marshall Key house in Washington in Mason County (lower right). The Kennedy plantation was said to have been the locale for her antislavery novel, which excited fervent interest in the North and angry reaction in the South and was regarded as largely contributing to the advent of the Civil War.

In his slave compensation claim (below), a "loyal citizen" of Kentucky seeks payment for a slave who had served in the U. S. Army.

CLAIM FOR COMPENSATION FOR ENLISTED SLAVE.

I, *Henry Harris*, a loyal citizen, and a resident of County of State of *Kentucky*, hereby claim compensation, under the provisions of section 24, Act approved February 24, 1864, and Section 2, Act approved July 28, 1866, for my slave *Anderson Arnett* enlisted 186 , at by in the *123 Infantry* Regiment U. S. Colored Troops Co. *B* certificate of enlistment, and a descriptive list, as required, accompany this application. That I did not acquire said slaves subsequent to said enlistment, but had a valid title to him at the date of said enlistment, and previous thereto: I having acquired my title to him and my ownership over him as follows, to-wit :

Slaveowners were continually troubled with runaway slaves who often were helped by the Underground Railroad in their efforts to reach Canada and freedom. The "railroad" was a secret network of agents and stations which spirited to the North hundreds of slaves from Kentucky and other southern states. Levi Coffin (above, left) was the reputed president of the railroad. The Reverend Calvin Fairbank (above, right) was an "agent" who served over seventeen years in the state penitentiary for helping fugitive slaves to escape. The Rothier House in Covington (below) was an important link in the railroad. A secret tunnel led from the house to the banks of the Ohio River, which the fleeing slaves crossed and then continued on their hazardous journey.

Slaves were sold either by private sale or at public auction, sometimes manacled with handcuffs and leg irons like those above. Slave traders at first conducted their business quietly so as not to arouse public indignation, but by the 1850s were bold enough to advertise in the Lexington newspapers. Prices of slaves varied according to their age, physical condition, sex, color, and skills. In the 1840s, prices ranged from $100 to $850 for female slaves and up to $2000 or more for highly skilled male workers.

Harriet Beecher Stowe is said to have witnessed the sale of several slaves at the old stone courthouse (right) in the village of Washington, Mason County, while she was visiting the Marshall Key family there. The incident is supposed to have been used in *Uncle Tom's Cabin*, which she wrote at her home in Brunswick, Maine after visiting Kentucky. Far from ridding Kentuckians of their proslavery views, the activities of outside abolitionists seemed merely to have aroused resentment and defensiveness on the slavery question.

The elderly couple from Mercer County (left) lived in Harrodsburg after the Civil War, where portly "Uncle" Iverson Wilkerson was the unofficial keeper of the pioneer burial ground at Fort Harrod. With Lucretia, his wife, the couple was set free after the Emancipation Proclamation of January 1863. Although no longer technically slaves, Kentucky blacks, like most of those in the South, lived in much the same conditions for several decades after the end of the Civil War. The family, shown below, probably experienced little change in their lives after emancipation.

Slavery was not without its opponents in Kentucky. Emancipation plans proliferated, though doomed from lack of public interest. Prominent among the abolitionists was Cassius Marcellus Clay, later Lincoln's ambassador to Russia, who while at Yale University was impressed by the teachings of William Lloyd Garrison. Some years later Clay heavily fortified a building in Lexington and in 1845 proceeded to publish an antislavery newspaper, *The True American*. The office was invaded by an angry mob, who boxed up the printing equipment and sent it to Ohio. A rare lithograph (above, left) shows Clay in 1846 at the height of his career.

The "Lion of White Hall" (above, right) at the age of eighty-four married the fifteen-year-old daughter of a tenant farmer. At right, Clay stands before his Madison County home.

Abraham Lincoln, the Great Emancipator, was born in Kentucky on his parents' farm near Hodgenville. The picture above is believed to be an authentic early photograph of the Thomas Lincoln cabin, now preserved as a national shrine.

An uncle of Thomas Lincoln, Joseph Hanks (upper left, with his wife) taught his nephew the trade of cabinetmaking. Hanks was a relative of Nancy Hanks, who later married Thomas.

The picture at the left of the young Abraham reading by firelight was done by Eastman Johnson, an American artist.

Religion

INDIFFERENCE to religion was a prominent feature of early frontier society. Preoccupation in Kentucky with the desperate effort to survive afforded many pioneers little time or interest for religious contemplation or affairs. Others celebrated their freedom on a new frontier by discarding all the restraints of civilization.

Not only western, but eastern society as well, was called "profane" by one observer, and many a despairing clergyman in the post-Revolutionary era agreed. In Kentucky's scattered settlements, however, there were Catholic, Presbyterian, Baptist, and Methodist congregations by 1800.

As the nineteenth century opened, an extraordinary religious fervor swept Kentucky, spreading across the frontier and then to all the South. The revival movement, born earlier in the

tending. The Great Revival had begun. As other liberal preachers joined, the meetings outgrew denominational limits and control. So enthusiastically did people respond that about 25,000 gathered in August, 1801 at the Cane Ridge Church (left) in Bourbon County to be exhorted by eighteen Presbyterian ministers and as many or more Baptist and Methodist preachers.

At these meetings the zeal of backwoods preachers often overcame prudence. Their highly emotional appeals to "sinners" to repent were answered in kind by their audience. Some listeners, overcome by excitement, can be seen prostrate in the pictures (left, and opposite page).

seaboard states, came to full bloom here as the Great Revival. To the Protestant churches it involved, this ambitious endeavor won thousands of new converts. It resulted in dissension and eventual schism as well.

The leader of the movement in Kentucky was the Reverend James McGready, a Presbyterian, who became pastor of three small Logan County churches in 1796. McGready's liberal ideas, powerful preaching, and popular revival techniques were readily accepted by frontiersmen who were unimpressed by theological arguments or rigid dogma. At some of the revivals, people attended from such distances that they camped overnight around the site. These events became known as "camp meetings," like that on the opposite page (lower left). They developed as a distinctive feature of the revival period.

This type of service became immensely popular on the frontier, where dispersed population, poor transportation, and great distances kept hardy ministers "living in the saddle" (right) in order to visit their flocks.

On the third Sunday in June 1800, McGready and his associates conducted an evangelistic meeting at his Red River Church with hundreds at-

The early clergymen faced overwhelming obstacles in ministering to their wilderness congregations. Like the Methodist circuit rider on the preceding page, traveling preachers braved the hardships of Indian attacks, weather, swollen streams, and lack of financial support. Of necessity, they were zealous, dedicated, and courageous.

From these pioneer preachers came a number of the revival leaders. Barton W. Stone (upper right), pastor of the Cane Ridge Church at the time of its huge revival in 1801, left the Presbyterian church in 1804 to found the Christian Church, another of the denominational split-offs resulting from the Great Revival.

Peter Cartwright (upper left), one of the most capable of the revivalists, joined the Methodist Church during the revival of 1801 and later spent four years riding the circuit in Kentucky.

Like other Catholic clergy, the Reverend Stephen T. Badin (left) strongly opposed revivals. As the first Catholic priest ordained in the United States, Badin came to the Western Country in 1793, and for several years was the only priest for all Kentucky.

The revival meetings produced thousands of conversions, and church membership grew. But the excesses of the revivals and of some of the revival preachers caused the more conservative clergy to denounce the once-promising endeavor.

Not everyone sought a religious experience at these events. The general excitement offered opportunity to thieves and to rowdies (below) who tried to break up meetings. Skeptics appeared with vinegar-soaked bread to stuff in the mouths of those who fell in religious ecstasy. Meanwhile, some "sinners" cried and shrieked for mercy as the preachers warmed to their subject. Others were possessed with strange uncontrollable jerking movements. It was said that the long unbraided hair of women seized with the wild movements would crack like a whip. Grown men and women crawled on hands and knees, barking like dogs.

As congregations grew and built permanent churches, formal worship and a better-educated ministry became more important. The camp meeting declined, after the fanaticism had flourished for over a decade. In 1885 a cultivated minister like the Reverend Henry Ward Beecher could draw large audiences for his lectures (see poster at right).

REV. HENRY WARD
BEECHER

Will deliver his world-famous Lecture,

"THE REIGN OF THE
COMMON PEOPLE,"
AT ODEON HALL,

Bowling Green, Ky., Friday Eve.,

MARCH 27th.

This will be the only place Mr. Beecher will Lecture at in Southern Kentucky, and this Lecture tour will be the last he will make.

PRICES OF ADMISSION:

Reserved Seats, $1; General Admission, 75 Cents; Gallery, 50 Cents.

Seats now on sale at T. J. SMITH & CO'S.

Doors Open at 7; Lecture at 8 o'clock, Sharp.

1885

The Cane Ridge Meeting House (above), scene of the famous revival of 1801, is now enclosed by a stone building. The Reverend Barton W. Stone began his ministry here in 1796.

Near Harrodsburg stands the Mud Meeting House (below), the first Dutch Reformed Church west of the Alleghenies, built around 1800. A portion of the mud-chinked walls, which gave the church its name and which were later covered with weatherboards, is visible.

Masterson's Station in Fayette County (above) was the site in 1790 of the first Methodist conference west of the Alleghenies with Bishop Francis Asbury presiding. The photograph above was taken one hundred years later—May 15, 1890.

Ministers of all denominations were free to use the Republican Meeting House (left) in Fayette County. Barton W. Stone was one of the pastors. The meetinghouse was built in 1817.

Old Mulkey Meeting House (above), near Tompkinsville, was built around 1798 by Baptist immigrants. One of the oldest log churches in Kentucky, the unusual structure has twelve corners, thought to represent either the Twelve Apostles or the Twelve Tribes of Israel. In the nearby burying ground are the graves of Daniel Boone's sister Hannah and many pioneers. The site is now a state shrine.

The Little Church on the Hill (left) near Covington was built in 1901 by Father Albert Soltis of the Order of St. Benedict and holds only three people. Monte Casino, the "world's smallest church," was built entirely of native limestone except for the small stained-glass window and the narrow door.

Built in 1801, Walnut Hill Presbyterian Church (left) is the oldest Presbyterian Church building in Kentucky. The church was organized in 1785 near Lexington, and the original log building stood close to this stone church.

Barton W. Stone, founder of the Christian Church, moved to Lexington in 1816, where he attracted several followers. The group bought a former cotton factory which they remodeled and dedicated in 1831 as Hill Street Christian Church (left, center). Here, in January 1832, the followers of Stone, called "Stoneites" and the adherents of Alexander Campbell, known as "Campbellites," united to form the present Christian Church (Disciples of Christ). One of the first Sunday schools of the Christian Churches in Kentucky was conducted here. By 1842 the congregation had outgrown the small church and moved. The church, in later years a double residence, has recently been razed.

The replica of the Red River Meeting House (lower left) recreates the site of the first camp meeting of the Great Revival in 1800 and the first church of any denomination in western Kentucky. Built around 1783, the original church was also associated with Finis Ewing, one of the founders of the Cumberland Presbyterian Church, another schism growing out of the Great Revival.

The revivals were over, leaving in their wake not only the western schisms but also a fundamentalism that continues to distinguish several denominations today.

The Primitive Baptist custom of foot washing (left) is a literal application of a New Testament passage. The preacher, girded with a long towel, washes the feet of the men in his congregation. The women's feet are washed by women. Baptizing by immersion in ponds (above and opposite page) has been practiced by fundamentalist churches.

Even before the revivals began, many western liberal Protestants disagreed with conservatives over doctrine and the amount of education to be required of the clergy.

Ministers had come west after the Revolution, but in such small numbers that they could not keep up with the rapidly growing population.

College-trained clergy were scarce and westerners were willing to lower drastically the standards for ordination. A candidate was judged on his zeal and his ability to preach convincingly, rather than on his erudition and his adherence to approved doctrine.

A literal, or fundamentalist, interpretation of the Bible appealed not only to these men but to their unsophisticated congregations as well.

A Presbyterian had introduced the revivals into Kentucky, and the Presbyterian Church suffered the most from them. Two new denominations—the Christian and the Cumberland Presbyterian—had come into being by 1810 as a result of the "camp meeting" revivals.

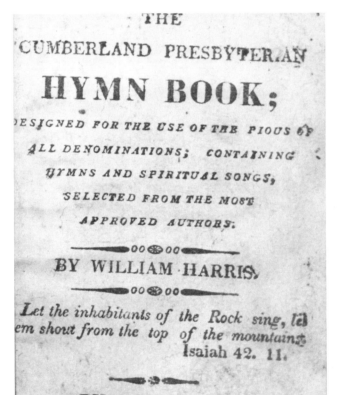

THE

CUMBERLAND PRESBYTERIAN

HYMN BOOK;

DESIGNED FOR THE USE OF THE PIOUS OF

ALL DENOMINATIONS; CONTAINING

HYMNS AND SPIRITUAL SONGS,

SELECTED FROM THE MOST

APPROVED AUTHORS.

BY WILLIAM HARRIS.

Let the inhabitants of the Rock sing, let them shout from the top of the mountains.
Isaiah 42. 11.

RUSSELLVILLE:

CHARLES RHEA, PRINTER.

1824.

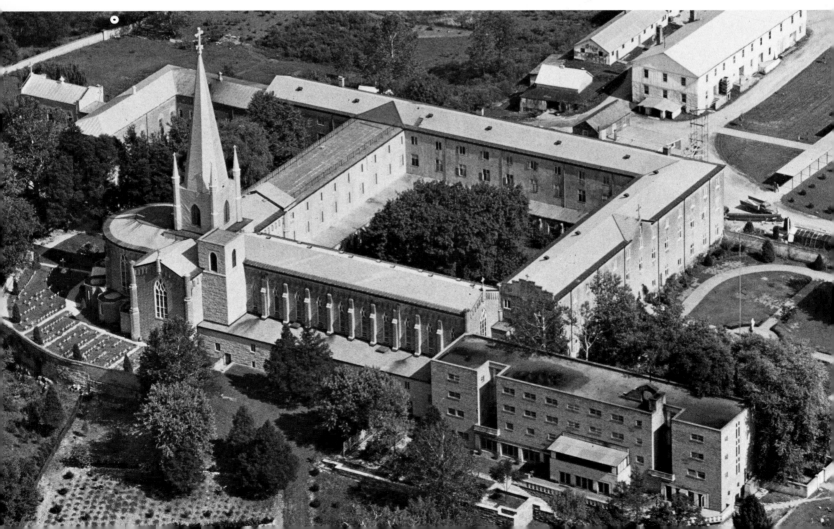

Neither the Catholic Church nor the Episcopal Church was affected by, or took part in, the revivals. Episcopalians organized as early as 1796 when the Christ Church congregation was formed in Lexington. The present Christ Church (right) was built in 1847. In the West, the church was hindered by its Anglican origin and the American distrust of anything English. Not until the last half of the nineteenth century did the church in Kentucky grow substantially in membership.

The Catholic Church from the beginning had such excellent leaders as Fathers Stephen Badin, Edward D. Fenwick, Charles Nerinckx, and Benedict Joseph Flaget, bishop of Bardstown.

Many of the early Catholic immigrants settled in central Kentucky, where the seat of the church government was located in 1808 at Bardstown. Here St. Joseph's Cathedral (upper right, opposite page) was consecrated in 1819, the first west of the Alleghenies.

A statue of Bishop Flaget stands before the cathedral (opposite page, far left). Within the church are century-old religious paintings, said to have been the gifts of Louis Philippe and other royal donors.

During the first half of the nineteenth century there existed several Orders of the Catholic Church in Kentucky: Dominicans, Jesuits, Benedictines, the Sisters of Loretto, and the Sisters of Charity of Nazareth. The Cistercians (or Trappists) arrived from France in 1844. Their monastery is at Gethsemani in Nelson County (opposite page, lower left).

Members of the diocese at Bardstown established the first seminary west of the Alleghenies in 1811 and in 1816 built St. Thomas Church (right), the oldest Catholic church building standing in Kentucky.

When the Bardstown diocese was outlined, its jurisdiction included Tennessee and the entire Northwest, as well as Kentucky. After it became apparent that Bardstown could not fulfill its earlier promise of growth, the Catholic See was moved to Louisville in 1841.

The wilderness tested those clergymen, both Catholic and Protestant, who dared to seek the expansion of religion into new areas. In return, they influenced a turbulent new society toward a higher degree of stability.

Shakers

E ARLY in the nineteenth century, Shaker missionaries established two of their utopian communities in Kentucky: South Union in Logan County, and Pleasant Hill in Mercer County. Shakers, so named from their fervent dancing during their worship, were a communal religious society that migrated to America from England in 1774. Under the leadership of Mother Ann Lee, their matriarch, they founded the first society in Albany, New York, and eventually sent out missionaries to New England and the West. In 1805 the intense religious excitement of the Great Revival attracted three Shaker missionaries to Kentucky, where they preached at first in Garrard County in March, 1805. Arriving in Logan County in 1807, they gathered converts and by 1811 for farming and orchards, in addition to that given by members. An ambitious building program (see map, right) called for mills, a meetinghouse, and family dwellings. Shakers, who took a vow of celibacy, were grouped into "families," or orders, men living on one side of the dormitorylike houses, and women on the other.

In its exaltation of work, the society did not exempt its leaders from the humblest tasks. Harvey L. Eades (above) was bishop of the two Kentucky societies, and also ox driver, shoemaker, tailor, teacher, farmer, author—among other occupations.

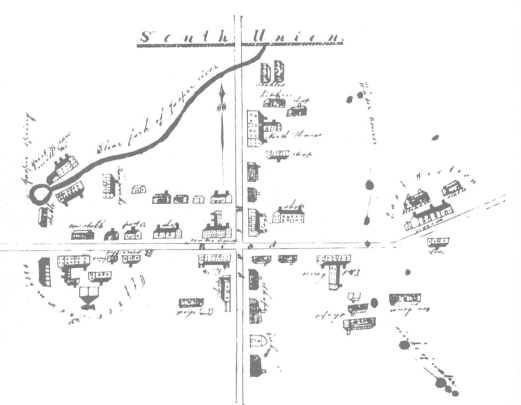

The first structures at South Union were of frame, but later brick was used, as in the Main Building (above).

With marriage forbidden, membership was maintained by winning converts from other faiths and adopting children from orphanages. Families with children also joined. Initiates, accepting the rules of the society, signed the agreement above. Industrious Shakers at South Union reached the peak of their prosperity in the 1840s and 1850s. The group below was photographed in 1882, after the community had begun to decline.

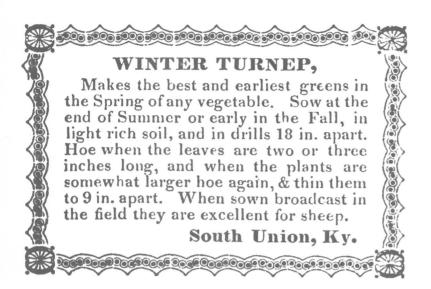

The Shakers were excellent farmers. Their principal sources of income were purebred cattle, canned fruit and preserves, and packaged herbs and garden seeds (above). Shaker sisters carried on a successful silk industry, from raising the silkworms to dyeing and spinning the thread. The much sought-after Shaker products reached increasing markets with the coming of the steamboat and railroad.

Skilled Shaker cabinetmakers produced furniture, such as the sewing table above and the dining room pieces below, which are still prized for their simplicity and beauty.

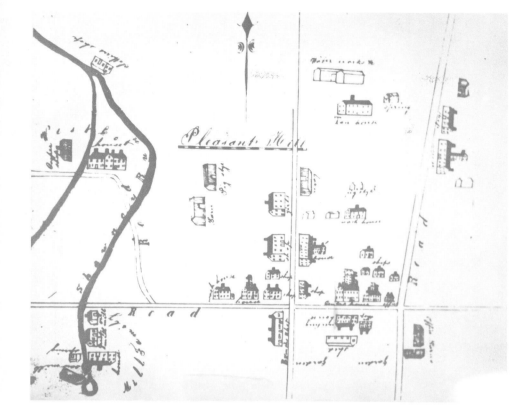

Shakers at Pleasant Hill formed their community in 1805, completing the first permanent building in 1809 (see map at left). By 1817 the first of the three principal family units had been organized, and the construction of the major family houses was undertaken. Between 1810 and the outbreak of the Civil War, the Kentucky believers developed a self-sufficient agrarian way of life. Their fertile, well-tended fields and gardens produced food for the village and a large surplus. Farm products left Pleasant Hill in the form of preserves, meal, flour, brooms, cured meats, rope, woven goods, and garden seeds. Like the South Union brethren, they raised and sold fine livestock. Nearly every sale of purebred sheep and cattle in Kentucky was attended by Shaker herdsmen in search of superior breeding stock.

Shakers, quick to use the newest in farm equipment, also had their own clever smiths and craftsmen who developed efficient implements and mechanical aids. Elder members, such as those at left, were given thoughtful care and assigned tasks according to their abilities.

A love of excellence found expression in their plain but attractively designed buildings. In the ranks of the Pleasant Hill Shakers was an architectural genius, Micajah Burnett, who joined the society as a young man of seventeen. The buildings at Pleasant Hill, especially the graceful spiral staircase in the Trustee's House (left), are lasting monuments not only to Burnett but to the aspirations of the Shakers themselves.

What is believed to be the first public waterworks west of the Alleghenies was built by the Shakers at Pleasant Hill. The water storage house (below) was part of the system. Horse power was used to pump water from a spring 1800 feet away to a large cypress tank in the water house. Mounted on stone piers, the tank has a capacity of 4400 gallons.

Dr. William Pennebaker, Pleasant Hill physician and a prominent Shaker, was photographed with a group of Shaker women (below left).

Women Shakers shared equally in managing the thriving community and in the administration of religious affairs. They were active participants in the various ceremonies and in the daily chores of cultivating gardens, spinning, weaving, sewing, preserving and canning, gathering herbs, and drying garden seeds. The room above, with its weaving implements, although photographed at Locust Grove in Louisville, might easily have been a typical Shaker workroom.

Sister Mary Settles (right), the last surviving member of the Pleasant Hill society, was a widow with several children when she joined the community. She taught school there for many years and died in 1923. By around 1910, the rich Shaker acreage had passed into other hands in return for the lifetime care of the last twelve remaining Shakers.

The beginning of the Shaker experiment in Kentucky had been promising and for about fifty years the two communities flourished. With the outbreak of the Civil War, however, the fortunes of the Shakers were reversed. The war brought hardships to the villagers, as opposing armies marched through Pleasant Hill and South Union. Both sides demanded food, forage, and fresh horses, doing severe economic damage. Guerrilla looting meant further losses.

The Shakers also suffered from the loss of older and more dedicated leaders, dissension, poor business management, and loss of markets. Never again after 1865 did the Shakers regain the prosperity and promise of the antebellum years.

Pleasant Hill was dissolved in 1910. South Union, the last of Kentucky's two colonies, closed in 1922. The Pleasant Hill restoration, which includes the Trustees' House, now used as an inn (above), and the museum in the Center Family House (below), truly preserves the character of the Shaker community.

V. THE CIVIL WAR

The boom of South Carolina's guns against Fort Sumter, the wave of secession among the southern states, and Lincoln's call for troops to put down the rebellion found Kentuckians torn by loyalties to both North and South. As a consequence the state's course during the conflict was wavering and uncertain.

Kentucky in 1861 was definitely opposed to secession. Since the War of 1812 the Commonwealth had had strong ties to the Union. In 1850 she had sent no delegates to the Nashville Convention called by southern representatives. A border state, Kentucky's trade across the Ohio and with southern markets had forged economic ties with both sections. And the many bonds of family and friendship cut across geographic boundaries.

The crisis split churches and communities, pitted fathers against sons, brothers against brothers—only natural perhaps for a state that could claim both Jefferson Davis (below, left) and Abraham Lincoln (below, right). In the end there was hardly a village that did not send men to fight on both sides.

Unwilling to commit itself, Kentucky proclaimed its neutrality in 1861, in effect leaving its citizens free to join either side. Recruiting camps on the borders—Confederate in Tennessee and Union across the Ohio from Louisville—were busy.

By August the neutrality proclaimed in May was being ignored by both sides. Recruiting went on openly. The "Stars and Bars" of the Confederacy vied with the "Stars and Stripes" of the Union. Soon Confederates occupied eastern Kentucky, Bowling Green, and Columbus, while Union forces took Louisville and Paducah. In September the Unionist-dominated legislature demanded a Confederate withdrawal and offered Brigadier General Robert Anderson command of Kentucky volunteers to accomplish it. Anderson, a native Kentuckian, had been the major in command of Fort Sumter when the guns of South Carolina opened fire on April 12, 1861.

In response, Confederate sympathizers from sixty-five counties formed a provisional government with its capital at Bowling Green. Kentucky was then accepted as the thirteenth state of the Confederacy. This move had little effect, for it lacked popular support, and federal military successes soon drove Kentucky's Confederate government into exile. Officially the state remained in the Union.

Fearful of losing the strategic advantage of controlling Kentucky, the North kept large numbers of troops here in what was virtually a military occupation. The photograph at right shows a provision and munition train passing through Maysville on its way to federal forces farther south. Ohio troops land at Louisville (below), headquarters of General Anderson.

Early in the war, on December 17, 1861, a spirited but brief engagement was fought at Rowlett's Station on the south bank of the Green River near Munfordville. In the scene at left the Union troops withstand a Confederate cavalry charge, one of the few times during the war that infantry skirmishers engaged cavalry in the open.

Although Kentucky was invaded a number of times, most engagements within her borders were minor. Sustained Confederate occupation ended early in 1862 when Albert Sidney Johnston withdrew from Bowling Green. Later that year, Kirby Smith advanced through Cumberland Gap toward Lexington, routing the federal troops at Richmond under William Nelson on August 30. At the same time, Braxton Bragg, in an attempt to "liberate" Kentucky, marched from southern Kentucky toward Lexington. His Confederate troops met those under the command of Don Carlos Buell at Perry-

ville, near Harrodsburg (October 8, 1862) in a bloody but inconclusive battle (below) that cost both sides some 1300 dead and 5400 wounded.

With the exception of John Hunt Morgan's cavalry raids, the major fighting was over in Kentucky. Confederate Nathan Bedford Forrest in 1864 advanced through western Kentucky to Paducah, but soon withdrew. Guerrilla activity, however, continued until the war was over and left a residue of bitter feeling especially in the mountains.

John B. Hood　　　*John Hunt Morgan*

Major General John C. Breckinridge (above) was one of the Kentucky officers who served the Confederacy with distinction, mainly in the West. Vice-President of the United States under James

Buchanan and secretary of war in the Confederate cabinet, he was acclaimed by Kentuckians after the war for his outstanding military record.

General John B. Hood, a native of Owingsville, commanded the Army of Tennessee and took part in the Atlanta campaign, replacing General Joseph E. Johnston.

Brigadier General John Hunt Morgan gained the name "Thunderbolt of the Confederacy" for his daring raids behind enemy lines.

General Leonidas Polk, an Episcopal Bishop, and his Confederates established the heavily-fortified "Gibraltar of the West" on the bluffs of Columbus, opposite Ulysses Grant's position across the Mississippi in Belmont. The six-ton anchor and links (right) were part of a mile-long chain stretched across the river to deter Union troop movements south. On the facing page, Union soldiers are shown landing on the Kentucky shore opposite Cairo, Illinois.

Simon Bolivar Buckner   *Albert Sidney Johnston*

Major General Simon Bolivar Buckner commanded the State Guard until Kentucky's neutrality ended. Commissioned by the Confederacy in 1861, he fought at Perryville and Chickamauga and later commanded the Department of East Tennessee and the District of Louisiana.

General Albert Sidney Johnston, commander of the Confederate Department of the West, retreated from Mill Springs and Forts Henry and Donelson, but never lost Jefferson Davis's support.

He died in the Battle of Shiloh in an attempt to rally his men.

Brigadier General Roger W. Hanson (above), "Old Flintlock," succeeded John C. Breckinridge as commander of the "Orphan Brigade" (1st Kentucky Infantry, CSA). He was killed at the Battle of Stone's River, Tennessee.

John W. Finnell   *Lovell H. Rousseau*   *William Nelson*   *Thomas J. Wood*   *Jeremiah T. Boyle*

Robert Anderson

The Union cause was also well served by Kentuckians such as Brigadier General Robert Anderson who during his brief command helped save the state for the Union.

John W. Finnell was appointed adjutant general in 1861 by Governor Beriah Magoffin.

Major General Lovell H. Rousseau established Camp Jo Holt for Union recruits and fought in several major engagements, including Perryville.

Brigadier General William "Bull" Nelson was sent to Kentucky by Lincoln to arm and to organize loyal troops. He established Camp Dick Robinson in Garrard County for Union recruits.

Major General Thomas J. Wood won the gratitude of Mississippi for his humane military administration of that state after the war.

Brigadier General Jeremiah T. Boyle was Kentucky's controversial military commander after the battle of Shiloh.

Ben Hardin Helm

Thomas L. Crittenden

George B. Crittenden

The two sons of John J. Crittenden illustrate dramatically the divided loyalties of Kentucky. Both became generals—Thomas L. Crittenden a major general in the Union army; George B. Crittenden a major general in the Confederate army.

Brigadier General Ben Hardin Helm, brother-in-law of Mrs. Lincoln, died leading his Confederate troops at Chickamauga.

Major General William Preston fought in several major battles and went on an abortive mission as Confederate minister to Mexico.

William Preston

Delegates from sixty-five counties held the Confederate Sovereignty Convention at the Coke-Clark house (near left) in Russellville in November 1861. They approved an act of secession, designated George W. Johnson provisional governor, and Bowling Green the capital.

The Battle of Logan's Crossroads, or Mill Springs, January 19, 1862 (far left), cost the life of Confederate General Felix Zollicoffer. Union troops, led by George H. Thomas, defeated the Confederates and opened the way into East Tennessee.

Kentucky and the Civil War

Places and Events

Cartography by T. P. Field and C. D. King

Cynthiana—Morgan was routed here on June 12, 1864 by a Union force four times greater than his own, and retreated back to Virginia.

Mt. Sterling—On his last raid into Kentucky John Hunt Morgan captured 380 Federals here on June 9, 1864. He then moved to Lexington and the foot soldiers he left behind were defeated by a surprise attack.

Brandenburg—Gen. John Hunt Morgan crossed the Ohio here to raid Indiana and Ohio, July 1863.

Richmond—Kirby Smith, advancing from Knoxville, defeated Gen. W. Nelson's Union forces and captured 4,303 on August 30, 1862.

Prestonsburg—Federals under Col. James A. Garfield attacked a Confederate force near here on Jan. 10, 1862. Both sides claimed victory.

Hodgenville—Abraham Lincoln born near here on Feb. 12, 1809.

Perryville—Here on Oct. 8, 1862 Confederate attempts to gain Kentucky came to an end. Bragg claimed victory over Buell, but it was not decisive.

Munfordville—The arrival of Bragg's main army here on Sept. 17, 1862 forced the union garrison in Munfordville to surrender and Bragg was now in the line of Buell's march. He moved east, possibly to join K. Smith, and thus Buell reached Louisville and reinforcements.

Paducah—Jumping off point for Grant's Mississippi Valley campaign.

Logan's Cross Roads—Federals under G. H. Thomas opened a path to eastern Tennessee.

Fairview—Jefferson Davis, Confederate President, born here on June 3, 1808.

Bowling Green—Headquarters of Gen. Albert Sidney Johnston, in charge of Confederate operations in the west. He was killed attacking Grant at Shiloh.

Columbus—Both North and South courted Kentucky and hesitated to make a hostile move. However, on Sept. 3, 1861, Confederate Gen. Leonidas Polk seized Columbus. Gen. U. S. Grant, in command at Cairo, Ill., countered by seizing Paducah. Kentucky was voted into the Confederacy at Richmond but never seceded from the Union.

Cumberland Gap—Occupied early in the war by Confederates. It served as a Confederate base throughout the conflict.

Troop Movements

MORGAN'S CAVALRY RAID—1863

Cartography by T. P. Field and C. D. King

Morgan continued northward to Salineville, which was the northernmost penetration of any Confederate troops. However, he was captured there and sent to prison in Columbus, from which he escaped by tunneling.

Louisville

Lexington

Brandenberg

Perryville

KIRBY SMITH—1862

Paducah

GRANT'S MISSISSIPPI VALLEY CAMPAIGN—1862

BUELL'S ROUTE TO PERRYVILLE—1862

BRAGG'S ROUTE

STONES RIVER—1862-63

TO PERRYVILLE—1862

STONES RIVER—1862-63

Cumberland Gap

Ft. Donaldson

Ft. Henry

From this point Grant continued southward to Shiloh and later, Vicksburg.

These two armies marched south to clash again at Murfreesboro, Tennessee.

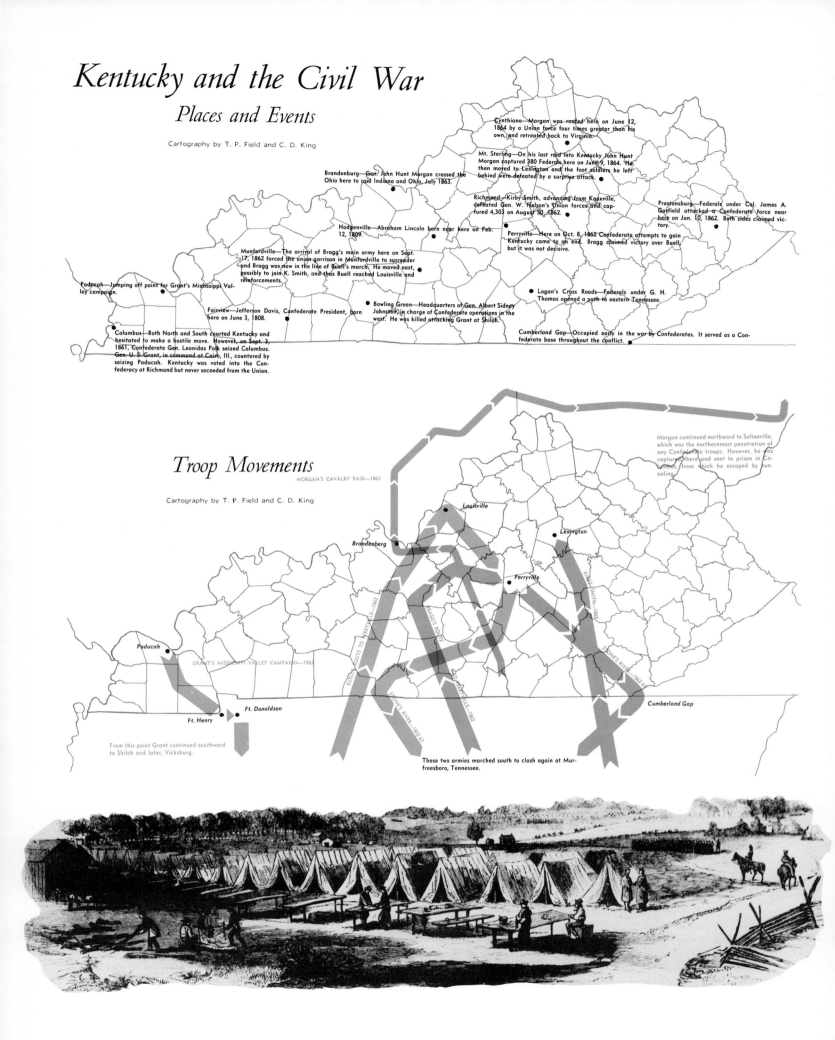

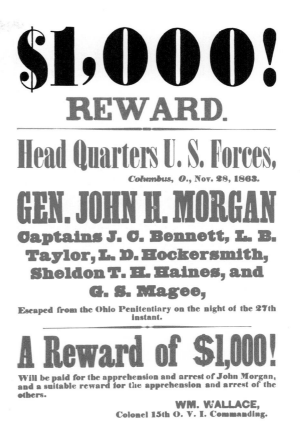

$1,000!
REWARD.

Head Quarters U. S. Forces,
Columbus, O., Nov. 28, 1863.

GEN. JOHN H. MORGAN
Captains J. C. Bennett, L. B. Taylor, L. D. Hockersmith, Sheldon T. H. Haines, and G. S. Magee,

Escaped from the Ohio Penitentiary on the night of the 27th instant.

A Reward of $1,000!

Will be paid for the apprehension and arrest of John Morgan, and a suitable reward for the apprehension and arrest of the others.

WM. WALLACE,
Colonel 15th O. V. I. Commanding.

The cry "Morgan's Raiders!" became a terrifying alarm to Unionists in Kentucky. Led by John Hunt Morgan (above, left), Confederate cavalry surprised federal soldiers at Cynthiana (left) on Morgan's first major raid into Kentucky in 1862. The next year Morgan was captured in Ohio, but escaped (see reward poster above) to lead his final disastrous raid in 1864. Treacherously surprised along about morning, Morgan ran from a house surrounded by federal troops and was shot and killed by a Union private in Greeneville, Tennessee, on September 4, 1864.

Union Camp Dick Robinson in Garrard County (far left).

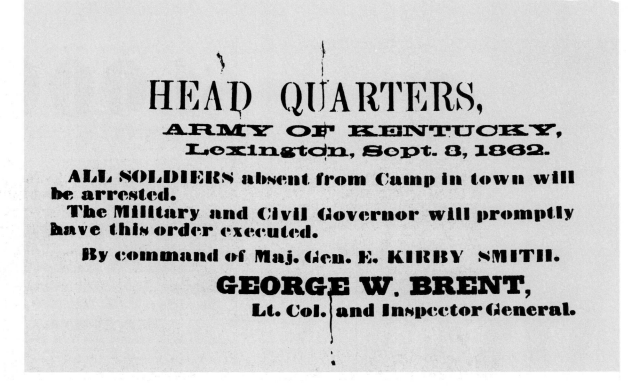

HEAD QUARTERS,
ARMY OF KENTUCKY,
Lexington, Sept. 8, 1862.

ALL SOLDIERS absent from Camp in town will be arrested.

The Military and Civil Governor will promptly have this order executed.

By command of Maj. Gen. E. KIRBY SMITH.

GEORGE W. BRENT,
Lt. Col. and Inspector General.

Although Kentucky remained in the Union, federal troops often treated it like a conquered territory. Arrests, sometimes of prominent citizens, were made without due process of law and on the barest suspicion of Confederate leanings. Scores of people were thrown into jail without indictment or trial, and many were sent to northern prisons.

Teachers and clergymen were required to submit to test oaths. The military interfered with elections and dominated the judiciary. Commercial restrictions were similar to those placed upon Confederate states, and "untrustworthy" or pro southern newspapers were suppressed.

Buell and his army enter Louisville (below).

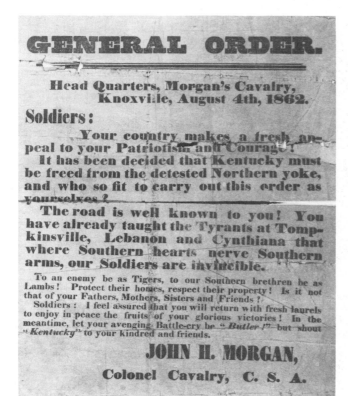

In the Jackson Purchase and in the Bluegrass, both areas of strong southern sympathies, military occupation was especially harsh. In the Purchase a number of civilians suspected of being guerrillas were summarily executed.

A Confederate attempt to exploit northern oppression may be seen in Morgan's general order (above), calling upon his men to free Kentucky from "the detested Northern yoke."

Kentuckians generally remained loyal, although Lincoln, represented in the cartoon below as declaring "No peace without Abolition!" drew their ire with his Emancipation Proclamation. An even greater outcry was raised over the Union decision to enlist Negro troops. On this issue the state was close to armed resistance. In the 1864 election Lincoln lost Kentucky by a margin of three to one.

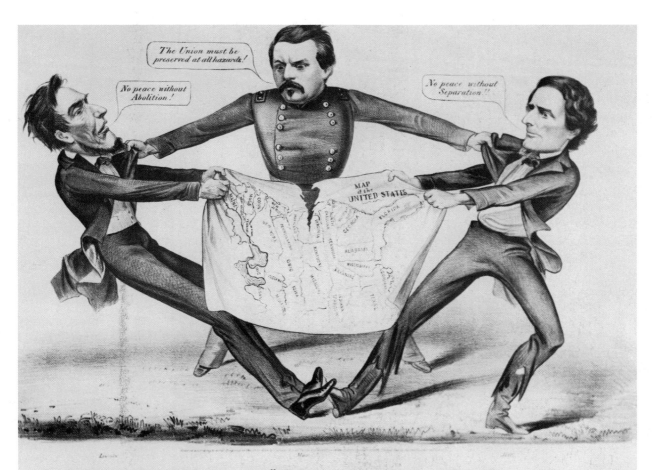

THE TRUE ISSUE OR "THATS WHATS THE MATTER".

Unresponsive to Bragg's attempt at "liberation" in 1862, Kentuckians after the war became enthusiastically pro-southern. This feeling was nourished by their resentment over the uncompensated loss of their slaves and the harshness of military occupation and by their sympathy with the suffering of the southern states under Reconstruction. So notable was the change that a Cincinnati paper complained that the state was as effectively controlled by the rebels as if they had garrisons in every town and city.

Reconstruction as known in the South hardly touched Kentucky. Rather, in the words of one historian, the period after the war was one of "readjustment," marked by a more democratic society as a result of the abolition of slavery, better distribution of land, and the rise of the business class.

Under the prosouthern Democratic party which largely controlled the state until 1880, Kentuckians strongly opposed the federal acts on behalf of Negroes, regarding them as violations of states' rights. Negroes did not vote until 1870, but the occasion was without violence.

Even as agriculture slowly recovered, men of vision were advocating a "new South" that would embrace industry and forget sectional differences. Through this period of change Kentucky profited by its course of moderation.

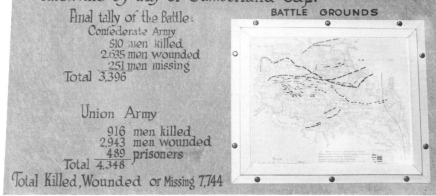

THE BATTLE OF PERRYVILLE

The Battle of Perryville was fought on October 7th & 8th, 1862 and was considered by many to have been the bloodiest campaign of the War between the States.

General Braxton Bragg and Leonidas Polk were in command of 16,000 Confederate Troops, and General Don Carlos Buell of the Union Army had 32,000 men in action.

On October 7th there was desultry fighting in order to gain possession of the only water supply in the vicinity.

On October 8th there was some skirmishing in the morning, but the battle did not begin in earnest until 2 O'clock in the afternoon. It raged fiercely until 7 O'clock in the evening. About midnight of the same day General Bragg withdrew and marched toward Harrodsburg. The following day, Buell's Army advanced toward this position, and Bragg prepared for battle on the Harrodsburg pike 8 miles from Perryville. No attack was made however, since Bragg suddenly determined to retreat to Knoxville by way of Cumberland Gap.

Final tally of the Battle:
Confederate Army
510 men killed
2,635 men wounded
251 men missing
Total 3,396

Union Army
916 men killed
2,943 men wounded
489 prisoners
Total 4,348

Total Killed, Wounded or Missing 7,744

BATTLE GROUNDS

MARTIAL LAW PROCLAIMED!

This town is declared under Martial Law. All citizens and soldiers except the guard, will retire to their quarters at 8 o'clock, P. M. A strong force will be stationed in the town. All persons found in the streets will be arrested.— Any one attempting to fire any building will be shot without trial.
W. J. HARDEE,
Bowling-Green, Feb. 13th, 1862.
Maj. Gen.

The birthplace of Confederate President Jefferson Davis, near Fairview in Todd County, is marked by this 351-foot concrete obelisk. Built during the years 1917-1924, it is the fourth tallest monument in the United States and the highest cast-concrete structure of its kind. An observation room near the top can be reached by an elevator. Close by is a replica of the house in which Davis was born on June 3, 1808.

This handsome granite and marble building shelters the log cabin in which Abraham Lincoln was born February 12, 1809. The cabin is on its original site on the Sinking Spring farm bought in 1808 by Lincoln's parents, Thomas and Nancy Hanks Lincoln. Fifty-six steps, representing the fifty-six years of Lincoln's life, lead up to the memorial building.

Sinking Spring, which gave the farm its name, can still be seen. An old oak boundary-line tree, a landmark at the time of the President's birth, still stands on the grounds of the park.

The shrine is in the Abraham Lincoln Birthplace National Historic Site, three miles south of Hodgenville in north central Kentucky.

VI. POLITICS

Kentuckians have relished politics since pioneer days. Frontier zest and a steady supply of stirring issues combined to produce an exuberant brand of politician who could find controversy even in the song, "Old Dog Tray," and be moved to grand heights of eloquence thereby.

From the ranks of Kentucky politicians have risen many leaders of national stature, including Henry Clay, Zachary Taylor, Abraham Lincoln, and Jefferson Davis.

Clay (below, left) and John J. Crittenden (right), both advocates of compromising the bitter slavery issue, early steered the state toward a course of moderation.

Political thought in Kentucky has never been overwhelmingly of a single conviction. If Jeffersonian Republican ideas appealed to many frontiersmen, there were others who embraced the aristocratic Federalist Party. As the Jeffersonian party declined, the Jacksonian Democrats and

Reception of the Remains of
HON. HENRY CLAY.

THE YOUNG MEN OF
LOUISVILLE,

(irrespective of party,) are requested to meet at the **COURT HOUSE**, this evening, at 8 o'clock, for the purpose of making arrangements to receive the Remains of Mr. **CLAY**, and to escort them to Ashland. It is hoped that every young man in the City will attend.

July 6, 1852.

Clay's Whigs increased. After the death of Clay, whose funeral cortege is shown at upper right, and the demise of the Whig party, the Know-Nothing movement enjoyed a brief popularity. The Democratic party, which vied for dominance with the Whigs during the 1850s, was split for a time by sectional differences, but after the Civil War it became Kentucky's leading party, with a strong pro-Confederate leaning. Not until 1895 were the more conservative Republicans able to elect their first governor, William O'Connell Bradley.

Richard M. Johnson (above), like Clay, supported an expansionist national policy, even advocating the annexation of Canada during the War of 1812. He was vice president under Martin Van Buren.

PUBLIC SPEAKING AND
BARBECUE.

On Friday, the 1st of July, at the Salt Spring, near Shaker Town, on the Kentucky River, the candidates of Woodford and Mercer will deliver addresses. Hon. T. F. Marshall and T. P. Porter, of Woodford, and all the candidates of Mercer, will be present. We also expect Hons. R. P. Letcher and J. C. Breckinridge, candidates for Congress in the 8th district, to be with us.

A Barbecue of fresh fish, mutton, shoat,&c., will be given by J W Hawkins, and at night a ball.

Strict attention will be paid to the guests in attendance by.--James W Hawkins, John S Overstreet, Dr Wm Coffey, R J Overstreet and S A Hawkins, Managers.

May 31st, 1853.

An occasion such as the "public speaking" in 1853 (above), with its inducements of a barbecue and ball, displayed the taste of Kentuckians for political spectacle.

Politics might be a serious matter, but Kentuckians could also laugh at the "facts and follies" of the day, as indicated in the political cartoon of the immediate post-Civil War period (below).

Adlai E. Stevenson (upper left) was vice president in Grover Cleveland's second term. At a rally in Jessamine County in 1944 (below), Senator, later Vice President, Alben W. Barkley ladles Kentucky burgoo. To left is Jim Looney, the Burgoo King.

The rare photograph above is of a trial after the 1900 assassination of William Goebel, Democratic candidate for governor. The bitter debate over the real winner resulted in a special election that year.

These Kentuckians have been appointed to the United States Supreme Court. With dates of their tenures, they are (from left, above): Thomas Todd, 1807-1826; Robert Trimble, 1826-1828; and John Marshall Harlan, 1877-1911. From left, below: Louis D. Brandeis, 1916-1939; Stanley F. Reed, 1938-1957; and Fred M. Vinson, 1946-1953.

Todd rendered not over a dozen opinions in his nineteen-year term, but was highly respected for them by his colleagues. Trimble, like Todd a Virginian by birth, succeeded Todd and died two years later. Harlan was a strong defender of civil rights and handed down decisions which were often ahead of his time, but later vindicated. Justice Brandeis, who in his law practice had earned a reputation as the "people's advocate," joined Chief Justice Oliver Wendell Holmes in a position of judicial liberalism. Reed had been general counsel of federal agencies before his appointment. Vinson, thirteenth Chief Justice, was noted for his support of a broad interpretation of federal governmental powers and for upholding the rights of racial minorities.

Four other Kentuckians have served on the nation's highest bench. Their names and years of tenure are: Samuel Freeman Miller (1862-1890), Horace Lurton (1910-1914), James Clark McReynolds (1914-1941), and Wiley Blount Rutledge (1943-1949).

The moonight falls the softest in Kentucky;
The summer days come oftest in Kentucky;

    .   .   .   .   .   .

The song birds are the sweetest in Kentucky;
The Thoroughbreds are fleetest in Kentucky;
Mountains tower proudest,
Thunder peals the loudest,
The landscape is the grandest—
And politics—the damnedest, in Kentucky.

Judge James H. Mulligan, Lexington attorney and United States consul to Samoa, summed up Kentucky politics in his humorous poem, reproduced in part above. Below is Kentucky's capitol building in Frankfort.

Judge Joseph Holt (above, right) was commissioner of patents, postmaster general, and Lincoln's secretary of war (to 1862). As judge advocate general, he presided at the trial of the Lincoln conspirators.

VII. AGRICULTURE

Fertile river basins and lush grasslands drew settlers to Kentucky—first to the gently rolling Bluegrass region where, after laboriously clearing the forests and canebrakes, they planted Indian corn, traditional soil opener of the frontier. Their efforts are symbolized by the plow (below) which belonged to Henry Clay, gentleman farmer of a later day.

The transition from subsistence to commercial farming was rapid; by 1800, Kentucky hogs and cattle were being driven back across the mountains for sale in the older settlements, and money crops such as hemp and tobacco had appeared. Hemp was to become the backbone of the state's agriculture, but Kentucky farming has remained diversified. Many new and improved crop plants have been introduced by Kentucky agriculturalists, among them the mild-flavored Bibb lettuce developed by Major John Bibb (right).

These implements once were considered progressive. The hand-operated drill (right) was used for planting grain. The picturesque method of threshing wheat (below) was photographed in the 1940s. The steam engine furnished power to the separator which could thresh around 1000–1200 bushels a day. The owner of the outfit charged about 25¢ a bushel and furnished all the necessary labor.

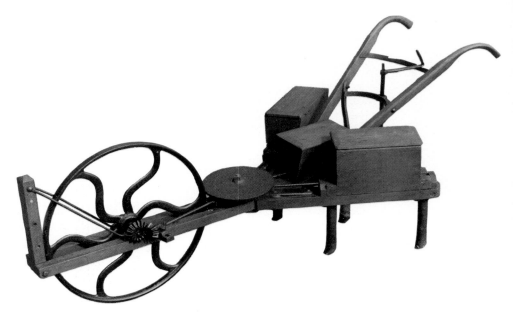

Cotton pickers (above) were once a common sight in The Purchase area of western Kentucky, where cotton is still grown on a large scale in five counties. The pickers dragged long bags behind them in the rows, filling them with cotton. From 200 to 225 pounds was considered a good day's work.

After the cotton is picked (usually by machines today), it is taken to a cotton gin such as the one below in Fulton County. Seeds are removed from the cotton, which is then compressed into 600-pound bales and covered with "cotton bagging." It is then ready for market. The bales are labeled, the top initials those of the landowner, and those below the tenant's.

Tobacco became the state's first major cash crop in 1787, when James Wilkinson negotiated with the Spanish for the privilege of shipping "tobacco, tallow, butter, well cured bacon, hams, lard and smoked briskets of beef" down the Mississippi to New Orleans.

With the decline of the market for hemp—of which Kentucky had been a leading producer—tobacco culture grew in importance, and by about 1912 to 1915 tobacco had supplanted hemp in the agriculture of the Kentucky River basin. In the years following World War I, manufacture of cigarettes increased, along with a demand for the milder white burley tobacco, which had been introduced into northern Kentucky about 1870. Kentucky tobacco production shot up by more than 50 percent in the decade after 1915.

The scene in Louisville (above) is a tobacco auction of the late nineteenth century. The cured tobacco, after being stripped, was compressed in a farmer's barn into large hogsheads and shipped to Louisville for sale. A sample or "hand" of tobacco was removed for the buyer's inspection. By the early 1900s, loose leaf tobacco auctions were being held in most central Kentucky towns and this replaced the older method of sale. The photograph below shows farmers bringing their tobacco to Lexington for sale about 1912.

This single-row setter (above) is used to reset young tobacco plants in the spring. Transplanting is one of many steps that lead to the tobacco warehouse in late fall.

Below, buyers for several large tobacco companies follow the auctioneer (third from left) in a Lexington warehouse. Each basket, usually 600 to 700 pounds of a certain grade, is sold separately.

Lexington today is the largest loose leaf tobacco warehouse center in the world.

Tobacco, shown in bloom at left, now represents over 53 percent of the value of all Kentucky crops, even with the sharp restrictions imposed by the federal regulatory program begun in 1933. Today, the value of a Kentucky farm is often determined largely by the size of its tobacco allotment.

For the tobacco farmer, the season begins with early spring plowing of the tobacco fields. The seedbed must be sterilized by firing, steaming, or fumigation. In March the beds are seeded and covered with tobacco canvas to protect the young plants from the sun and early frost. Plants are set out in fields in late May or early June, and weeds must be hoed and plowed throughout early summer. Blossoms and suckers are topped, or cut off, in late August or early September.

Several weeks later, the ripened plants are cut and hauled to barns where they cure through early fall. The bent barn, with its louvers for controlled ventilation of the curing leaf, is the characteristic farm structure of the area. The barn shown above is near Frankfort.

The final step, marketing, lasts from late November through early February. For most Kentucky farmers, the chant of the auctioneer spells success or failure for the year's operations.

The Knott County farmers plowing with steers (above) in the 1940s are reminiscent of the pioneer's use of oxen for the same purpose. The grain mill in the photograph at upper right was turned by a horse hitched to the pole which rotated the stones.

Oxen and milk cows for domestic use were brought by the pioneers to Kentucky, but beef cattle were not common until the 1790s. High-grade cattle appeared in Clark County in 1785 when the sons and a son-in-law of Matthew Patton introduced some of the elder Patton's imported English cattle. Patton brought the rest of the herd from Virginia several years later when he also emigrated to the Bluegrass.

Lewis Sanders and Henry Clay imported more purebred English cattle in 1817. For several decades livestock was emphasized in the state's agriculture. Just before the Civil War the state ranked fifth in the Union for the value of its livestock. Today it ranks third in the number of horses and mules, twelfth in swine, eighteenth in cattle and twentieth in sheep.

An auction of farm equipment (below) is usually held when a farmer goes out of business or sells his farm. At such a sale his old farming tools, livestock, implements, and often the household furniture will be offered to the highest bidder. Today the horse collar being held up before the crowd might be snapped up eagerly by an antique collector.

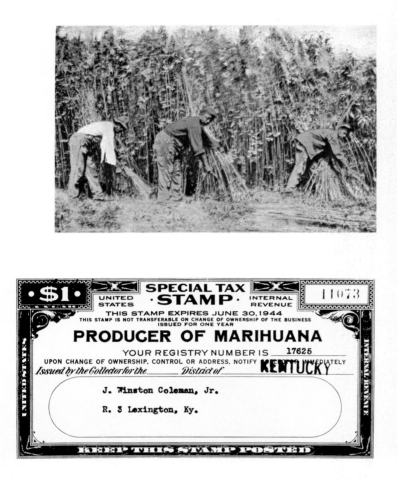

SPECIAL TAX STAMP

• $1 •

UNITED STATES · STAMP · INTERNAL REVENUE

11073

THIS STAMP EXPIRES JUNE 30, 1944
THIS STAMP IS NOT TRANSFERABLE ON CHANGE OF OWNERSHIP OF THE BUSINESS
ISSUED FOR ONE YEAR

PRODUCER OF MARIHUANA

YOUR REGISTRY NUMBER IS ___17625___

UPON CHANGE OF OWNERSHIP, CONTROL OR ADDRESS, NOTIFY **KENTUCKY** IMMEDIATELY

Issued by the Collector for the_____ District of_____ **KENTUCKY**

J. Winston Coleman, Jr.

R. 3 Lexington, Ky.

KEEP THIS STAMP POSTED

Kentucky was a leading producer of hemp (top picture) until about the first decade and a half of the twentieth century. During World War II, the federal government issued permits, like the one above, urging farmers, as a war measure, to grow hemp which was used in making burlap sacks, cotton bagging, oakum, rope, and twine. The editor of this book was among the Bluegrass farmers who raised hemp after this country's jute supply from the Philippine Islands was cut off.

At right, the worker is breaking hemp on a large Fayette County farm in the 1940s.

100

Whether bluegrass was native to Kentucky or a transplant brought in by the earliest settlers is a matter of conjecture. At any rate, today Kentucky bluegrass (*Poa pratensis*) is famous and the seed is in much demand for lawns and pastures.

Most of the seed is grown within a radius of twenty-five to thirty miles of Lexington in the heart of the Bluegrass region. The seed first must be stripped, as in the photograph above, which shows an old fashioned mule-drawn stripper. One man drove the horse or mule. The second man in the "box" below constantly raked the seed to the rear after it had been caught on a metal comb running the length of the vehicle. The bluegrass seed is sewed into large burlap sacks (left). The sacks of cured seed then are loaded on trucks, ready for market (above, center).

VIII. INDUSTRY

THE INDUSTRIES to be found in Kentucky are as varied as the Commonwealth's tremendous resources. Some have their origins in Kentucky's pioneer past, others are relative newcomers to a state blessed with natural wealth that encouraged industry from the beginning. World-famed Kentucky country hams, below left, are salted and sugared and hickory smoked before they are sold at the end of a year-long curing process. The early photograph of a Grayson County oil well (below) is a reminder that one of the first oil wells in the United States was drilled in the Commonwealth near Burkesville in 1829. Oil was accidentally discovered by Doctor John Croghan while he was drilling for salt water near the bank of the Cumberland River. The well was neglected for many years until the medicinal quality of the oil was discovered.

Once necessary to the self-sufficient pioneer life, folk arts developed into an interesting segment of Kentucky industry. In the old photograph at left, a woman weaves a wool coverlet on a loom. These coverlets were made commercially in the late 1890s.

Virgin forests, which produced trees six to eight feet in diameter, invited a logging industry that thrives today.

Workmen on the flat-bottomed boat used for supplies and shelter (above) prepare to escort a raft of logs down the Kentucky River. Logs were floated from the mountains down the river to Frankfort and other sawmill towns in early days.

In eastern Kentucky, this set of wheels with concave rims (left) was used to transport giant logs along a "railroad" made of smaller logs.

103

Before white settlement, Kentucky was heavily forested except for the thin soil of the knobby uplands. Even poorer soils could support a sparse stand of timber. To the farmer eager to get his land cleared for crops, the trees were a nuisance. The value of the woodland was soon realized, however, and the lumber industry became a major source of farm income.

As lumber supplies in a given area dwindled, sawmill operations such as the one above moved from place to place. This "groundhog," or portable sawmill, was located in eastern Kentucky.

Logs floating downriver have long been a familiar sight on the Kentucky, Green, Tradewater, Cumberland, and Tennessee. But the construction of locks and dams has caused this means of transporting logs to disappear almost entirely. The 500- to 600-foot length of these rafts made them too long to be successfully "locked" through the dams in one unit.

The log rafts (right) are being gathered at the confluence of the Tradewater and the Ohio, heading downriver to veneer plants. A small tugboat is used for speed and control.

Log rafts were held together by whalin' (strips of hickory twenty to twenty-five feet long) and raft pins. The pins were about ten inches long, round and sharp at one end. Today chains are used more often than whalin' or hickory raft pins.

The first applications of Kentucky water power in the 1800s were mills in which corn or other grains were ground. Soon after Harrodsburg and Boonesborough were settled, grist mills were built. The mill at left was built in 1877 on the site of an 1818 grist mill, and was in use until recent years at Mill Springs in Wayne County. The overshot wheel, powered by water from eight springs, turns at three and one-half revolutions a minute.

King's Mill on the Dix River (below) was submerged when Herrington Lake was formed in 1925. The mill, which had gears and machinery made of well seasoned hickory, stood near a covered bridge in Boyle County.

The old water mill (above) and the charcoal-burning iron blast furnace (below) represent two phases of Kentucky industry that flourished in the nineteenth century, then dwindled. The mill and its log dam stand on Troublesome Creek in Breathitt County.

When this unique double iron furnace was built in 1869, a town was chartered nearby in honor of the builders, Frank and Fred Fitch. Fitchburg, in Estill County, included mills, shops, a school, and homes for more than 100 families employed in operating the furnace. Nearly 10,000 tons of pig iron were produced in 1871. Kentucky at that time ranked seventh in the nation in iron production, one of the state's early industries.

The old photograph at left shows a blast furnace with its many outbuildings. The shed in the foreground is the "cast house" where the molten iron was drawn off and cast into "pigs." The furnace proper is at left front, topped by the "bridge house," from which the furnace was charged.

Ovens for producing coke (below) were built in the early 1900s on Rockhouse Creek in Letcher County.

By the mid-1880s, the once abundant supply of iron ore and hardwood timber for charcoal had been depleted, and most of the furnaces went out of blast. The ones remaining, which ranked Kentucky third among the iron-producing states in 1840, now stand as deserted stone stacks.

The leaching vats in Mammoth Cave (above) are the last reminder of a process that extracted saltpeter for making gunpowder during the War of 1812.

During the 1920s, horses were still pulling ice delivery wagons in Lexington, although trucks were rapidly gaining popularity for hauling and farm work. Note streetcars at left and in the background.

Wooden forms and nostalgic memories are all that remain of saltpeter-making and delivery of ice by horse-drawn wagons.

Coal, one of Kentucky's most valuable natural resources, is taken from the ground in underground mines or in surface mining operations. The eight-story shovel (left) is used to surface mine coal in Muhlenberg County. The bucket of the giant shovel can hold two large dump trucks parked side by side. For comparison, note the man and car in the lower right hand corner.

The story of the internationally known "Louisville Slugger" baseball bat (below left) began in 1884, when John Andrew Hillerich, son of a noted wood turner, offered to make a new bat for Pete Browning, star of the Louisville Eclipse team of the American Association. "The Old Gladiator" had just broken his favorite bat in a game and the young man, with Browning looking over his shoulder, produced the bat the star used when making "three for three" the next day.

Today the Hillerich and Bradsby firm is the recognized leader in production of baseball bats. Major leaguers of the past (Babe Ruth, Ty Cobb, Ted Williams) and of the present have relied on custom-made Sluggers.

Both locally based companies and firms head-quartered outside the state have contributed to the Commonwealth's economy. The early iron and steel works (above) is the largest in Kentucky and the forerunner of processing plants that have made Ashland one of the national centers of iron and steel production.

General Electric's Appliance Park outside Louis-ville (right) is the firm's largest producer of house-hold appliances.

There was no important commercial production of oil in Kentucky before 1880, although oil was struck as early as 1819. After the 1916 discovery of oil on Tick Fork of Cow Creek near Irvine, "wild-cat" oil prospectors came to the unproved fields of Kentucky. The finds were not as spectacular as those being made at the same period in the South-west, but the shallower oil sands here required less capital for drilling a well.

Ashland Oil and Refining Company began as a subsidiary of a company producing crude oil, but within twelve years Ashland was the main oper-ation.

The company's story began in 1918, when an Oklahoma oil promoter formed a corporation to produce Kentucky crude oil. Six years later the Swiss Oil Corporation financed the Ashland Refining Company, predecessor of the present firm.

Even in an expanding industry, the growth of Ashland Oil was remarkable in a field dominated by huge companies. Its assets grew from $250,000 at its founding in 1924, to $175,000,000 in 1956.

An Ashland oil refinery is at left. The giant petroleum tanks below are the terminus of thousands of miles of unseen pipelines.

Transportation of finished industrial products or of raw materials is often a dramatic story in itself, involving sometimes several types of carrier to reach a given destination. Coal on the freight cars (right) is emptied onto the waiting river barges.

Located within 500 miles of two-thirds of the population of America, Kentucky is an ideal site for processing plants of various kinds such as the refinery at right.

At Lexington, International Business Machines Corporation makes IBM typewriters and other office equipment in the plant at right. This is headquarters for the firm's office products manufacture, research, and sales.

Long before IBM chose to manufacture electric typewriters at Lexington, a small nail factory was established there on Town Branch creek. It was, some say, the first nail factory in America.

Today tiny pioneer industries have been succeeded by corporations of every size, including such giants as Westinghouse, Proctor & Gamble, and General Electric. Industrial sites such as the complex at Calvert City (below) offer pleasant and economical homes for industry.

Mining

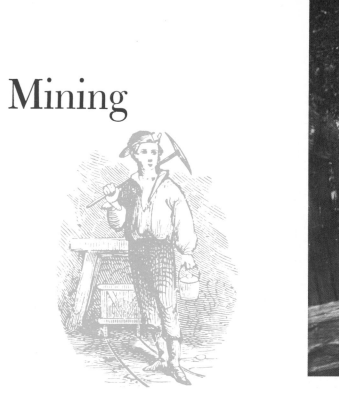

Mining is big business in Kentucky, third largest coal-producing state in the nation, second in fluorspar, and first in certain kinds of clay. Petroleum, natural gas, stone, sand and gravel are also important. But coal alone accounted for roughly three-fourths of the annual half-billion-dollar value of mine products in the late 1960s.

Coal is found both in eastern Kentucky's high-grade bituminous Appalachian fields and in the western part of the state. Before the Civil War, production centered in the western fields. Between 1880 and 1905, "rights" buyers came to eastern Kentucky to secure the mineral rights from mountain landowners, like those above, in long-term contracts, many of which are still in effect.

In early shafts such as the Elkhorn Field mine in Letcher County (opposite page, below), the mining methods were crude. The Gaines Coal Company's use of rails and mule power (above, right) was a step toward mechanization and easing the arduous labor demanded by coal mining.

Even after the arrival of the railroad, however, miners were still using horse- or mule-drawn carts to haul coal along portable tracks to the top of the tipples (below), where the coal was graded and emptied into waiting railroad cars. Production in Kentucky increased slowly, but in 1879 the state recorded its first million-ton year.

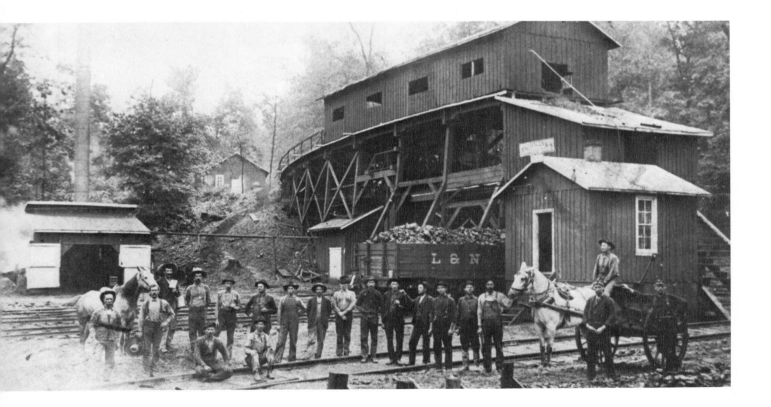

As mining techniques and equipment improved, production rose. Candles and Dutch lamps gave way to oil and carbide lamps; steel wedges and sledges yielded to hand drills and scrapers. The miners above, wearing electric lamps on their caps, load coal in a seven-foot seam in eastern Kentucky.

In the early 1900s, the railroad came into the eastern Kentucky fields (opposite page, upper right). Using modern equipment, mines boosted the state's production to nearly 39,000,000 tons in 1920, fourth in the country.

Coal Mining in Kentucky
Underground Mining

• Sites of underground mines.
General area of coal deposits.

Cartography by T. P. Field and C. D. King.

Regulations that require coal companies to reclaim surface-mined land have been enacted by the Kentucky Legislature to prevent such devastation as that, pictured at left, in the Rock Creek watershed. Little vegetation will grow on the barren subsoil turned up to reveal the coal, while acid and mud slides pollute the streams.

Coal Mining in Kentucky
Surface Mining

• Sites of auger and strip mines.

General area of coal deposits.

Cartography by T. P. Field and C. D. King

Three railroads—the Louisville and Nashville, Chesapeake and Ohio, and Norfolk and Western—combined efforts to lay tracks through eastern Kentucky. A new future opened for mining the day in April, 1915, when the first full train load of coal—thirty-three cars—left a Hazard mine for Milwaukee (right).

Supplied with electric power, mines now use electric carts (below) to help speed production and meet the heavier demand for eastern Kentucky coal created when the railroads provided an economical means of transportation.

The coal mining industry has had its problems. Frequent accidents have plagued miners, and as recently as 1970 thirty-six were killed in a Leslie County mine. The most significant labor difficulties occurred in 1931 when pitched battles were fought between scores of unionized miners and company-hired sheriff's deputies in eastern Kentucky. Mine employment has dropped because of competition from other fuels and the widespread use of mining machines.

Surface mining has been most widely used in the western fields, where some of the largest machinery used in mining is operated. But the terrain in the mountainous eastern regions makes the practice more difficult and more destructive (left and below). The opposition to the havoc it leaves behind has resulted in successively stricter laws to control surface mining and insure reclamation.

Transportation

THERE WAS no easy way for the earliest settlers to reach their "promised land" across the Appalachians. One route to Kentucky was by water, down the Monongahela and Ohio rivers to Limestone (Maysville). The other, the Wilderness Road, passed through Cumberland Gap in the southeastern corner of the state and wound along an ancient buffalo trace and Indian trail into the Bluegrass region. In the early days each had its dangers and difficulties.

Transportation was of vital interest to Kentuckians. By the mid-1790s they were improving the early trails for wagons by felling trees and rounding off the stumps. Over swampy places "corduroy" roads were sometimes built with logs laid crosswise and covered with a thin layer of dirt that soon washed away. At best these were makeshift improvements, and the pioneers' conveyances must indeed have been "jolt" wagons.

Transportation in the early twentieth century still involved animals, especially in the mountains. A team of sixteen oxen (above) was used to haul a large boiler over a winding mountain road.

Even as late as the 1940s rural families in eastern Kentucky (left) often went to town in a wagon.

Rural mail was delivered in this "all-weather" wagon (below) in central Kentucky between 1900 and 1925. Carrying the mail was only part of the job. The carrier might shop for the housewives in town; he conveyed messages and often exchanged news and gossip along his route.

Privately-owned turnpikes existed until around 1900, when counties bought them and opened the roads to free travel. Scrip (above) was often used during the Civil War to pay for passage on central Kentucky turnpikes.

The toll gate house on the Harrodsburg Pike near Lexington (above) was the only one of its kind in Kentucky. The traveller passed beneath the house; if he tried to sneak by without paying, the gatekeeper would let down the gate pole in time to rip off the buggy top. Funeral processions, doctors, and preachers traveled free.

Rivers with which Kentucky was so bountifully supplied became highways for many settlers. Some floated family and goods on flatboats (below) down the Ohio to Limestone (Maysville). From thence they might use "Smith's waggon-road" to central Kentucky. The unneeded boats were often broken up and used to build "flat-boat" houses.

The produce of the developing region began to move down the rivers, at first in canoes and pirogues, then on rafts, flatboats, and keelboats. The pole boat (upper left) could be slowly driven upstream by men pushing poles against the bottom or sides of a river, but carried only a small amount of freight.

The steamboat, beginning in the 1810s, made the river routes more useful. Navigability was improved by means of locks and dams on some major rivers and steamboats were designed for passage in shallower waters.

The "bat-wing" freight boat (third from top) drew only a foot and a half of water. These boats carried passengers and many kinds of merchandise up the Cumberland and Big Sandy to eastern Kentucky before the day of railroads and state highways.

Many of the pre-Civil War steamboats were sidewheelers, but sternwheelers like those at the wharf in Paducah (below) predominated in the late nineteenth century.

Electric interurban cars, which were common in the United States during the early part of this century, served a number of Kentucky cities: Louisville, Ashland, Frankfort, Paris, Georgetown, Nicholasville, Versailles, and Lexington. Ashland and Louisville expanded interstate connections to West Virginia, Ohio, and Indiana.

The car in the foreground (lower right) is one of the interurbans that ran from Lexington to five other central Kentucky towns between 1902 and 1934. Behind the interurban is a city street car, which was a successor to the early mule car of the 1880s (upper right) on Lexington streets.

Competition from busses and automobiles helped hasten the end of the interurban systems in the 1930s.

Developments in the Kentucky Rail Network Since 1865

Routes developed by 1865 and still in use.
Routes abandoned between 1865 and 1970.
Routes developed and abandoned between 1926 and 1970.
Routes developed between 1865 and 1926 and still in use.
Routes developed after 1926.

Cartography by T. P. Field and J. Fairchild

The railroad promised to solve many transportation problems when the Legislature chartered the Lexington and Ohio Company in 1830. Five years later, Lexington and Frankfort were connected by rail. The greatest development of rail facilities in Kentucky, however, came after the Civil War. By the late 1920s, there were about 4000 miles of tracks in the state.

The Cincinnati Southern Railroad's "Royal Palm," a crack passenger train, is shown at left on the last run of a steam locomotive on that line in Kentucky (about 1950). Diesel locomotives soon replaced the "iron horses."

Railroading was not without its mishaps. The wreck below occurred in 1895 when a wooden bridge in Marshall County collapsed beneath the steam engine and baggage car.

Only one Dewabout (above) was made, designed and manufactured by Thomas B. Dewhurst in Lexington (1899-1900). The more successful "Lexington" (below), manufactured in the city around 1909-1910, came in fifth of forty-seven cars entered in the southern Glidden Tour, a cross-country run.

Aviation was the last arrival on the transportation scene. Kentucky's first recognized airport, Bowman Field, was a pasture on the outskirts of Louisville in 1919. Unscheduled passenger service began there in 1924, followed by an air mail connection in 1925 and scheduled passenger service to Cleveland in 1927—the same year Bowman became a municipal field.

Shown above is the famous Curtiss NC-4, the first plane to cross the Atlantic, on a flight down the Ohio River in November, 1919.

By contrast, the swinging bridge in Breathitt County (below) is a good example of those footbridges privately built by mountain communities to connect their houses with the highway. Many are still in use today.

Covered bridges, once familiar sights on Kentucky's rural roads, gave shelter to travelers during summer showers, afforded shadowy seclusion where rural lovers might exchange kisses, and were a convenient place to post advertisements for patent medicines, circuses and public announcements. Many of them served for well over a century, and people alert to Kentucky's past are trying to preserve those still in existence.

The one at right is across the Chaplin River in Washington County. The wooden bridge at Frankfort (below), torn down about 1897, was replaced with the present "singing bridge." The interior view (near right, opposite page) shows the sturdy construction of the Ruddles Mill bridge in Bourbon County.

After World War II came an enormous expansion of automobile, bus, and truck traffic. Limited-access, four-lane highways in the form of state-financed toll roads began to be built in the 1950s, followed by the federal interstate highway system in the 1960s. In the midst of this modernization older services, like the Valley View Ferry (above, right) between Fayette and Madison counties, continues to help people get from one place to another.

Air travel has expanded spectacularly, while the railroads have almost eliminated passener service, though moving massive amounts of freight. Kentucky's rivers still carry a heavy tonnage.

IX. EDUCATION

WHEN Mrs. William Coomes in 1775 gathered the settlers' children at Fort Harrod to teach them elementary lessons, she established Kentucky's first school. Lacking books, John May taught from memory in 1779 at McAfee's Fort. Lexington's first teacher, "Wildcat" John McKinney, barehandedly fought a wildcat that invaded his one-room school on Cheapside.

The attitude of Kentucky's early settlers was influenced by the English tradition of private education, the relative rarity of colleges in the South, and the ease with which one could move up the social and economic ladder through agriculture and trade without formal training. Their reluctance to pay taxes and occasional "hard times" made the support of public education difficult. As a result, for more than a century after Mrs. Coomes' early classes, private academies and female seminaries were the nucleus of primary and secondary education in Kentucky.

William Holmes McGuffey (below), compiler of the *McGuffey Eclectic Readers* which sold an estimated 122,000,000 copies, was headmaster of an academy in Paris, Bourbon County, for several years.

Colonel Richard M. Johnson, reputed slayer of Tecumseh and later vice president of the United States, operated the Choctaw Academy, an Indian school (left and below) in Scott County in the 1830s.

Private academies and a few county academies prepared students for college and university work.

The Western Military Institute in Henry County (below, center) was first established at Georgetown in 1847 and offered courses leading to the bachelor and master of arts degrees.

The oldest Catholic college in Kentucky, St. Mary's, was founded in 1821 near Lebanon in Marion County. It now trains young men for the priesthood.

This quarter ticket entitles the holder to admission to the Third Gift Concert authorized by the Legislature of Ky. for the purpose of establishing in Louisville, Ky. a Library to be called The Public Library of Kentucky, forever free to all citizens of every state and also entitles the holder to one fourth of any gift awarded at this concert to whole ticket number.

135614   AGENT PUB. LIB. KY.

The Commonwealth early in its history allocated public lands to counties for financing education, but the proceeds usually went to private academies. By the 1820s, many local jurisdictions resorted to their own resources for setting up public schools.

One-room village schools of the nineteenth century looked much like the one pictured at right in Glensboro, Anderson County.

Even a venerable institution like the University of Louisville (top of page), the oldest municipally owned university in America, found its early expansion restricted by uncertain financial support. The University consisted of a school of medicine and a school of law until 1907, when a College of Arts and Sciences was added.

A lottery (opposite page) was the means adopted to obtain funds for the Louisville Free Public Library after the Civil War. The Library, founded in the eighteenth century, received its main impetus from the proceeds of the lottery.

The first free transportation for school children was provided by this "bus" (left) in Mason County in 1908.

State taxation for the support of education was made compulsory in 1904. By the time the commencement exercises of 1910 were held at the University of Kentucky (below), public education had come into better times.

Denominational colleges provided most of the higher education in Kentucky until the twentieth century.

Transylvania University, in Lexington, dating from 1780, was a denominational school but received state aid. The Main Building (right) burned in 1829. Cassius M. Clay, a student on the third floor, wrote in retrospect: "My black servant stuck a tallow candle to the steps in blacking my boots—went to sleep—& the flames went up like powder.... No one was lost as the fire began at the top."

Old Morrison (above) is the crowning architectural jewel of Transylvania. The Greek Revival brick building was designed by Lexington architect Gideon Shryock. It was completed during 1833-1834, after construction was interrupted by the 1833 outbreak of cholera.

Centre College (Presbyterian), at Danville, was chartered in 1819. "Old Centre" (above) was built in 1820 and is the oldest college building west of the Alleghenies and south of the Ohio.

Augusta College (Methodist), at Augusta in Bracken County, lost its charter in 1849 because of the college's participation in the anti-slavery movement. Kentucky Wesleyan, formerly in Millersburg and Winchester, is now located in Owensboro.

Georgetown College (Baptist) at Georgetown was founded in 1829.

Berea College, interdenominational institution in Madison County, was established in the 1850s to train Appalachian youth and Negro students. Phelps-Stokes Chapel is at left.

Early colleges in Kentucky were private, created and supported by the various religious denominations. There was bitter opposition to the state-supported, nonsectarian Agricultural and Mechanical College of Kentucky in Lexington. In 1916 it became the University of Kentucky, which today is a sprawling multi-system including thirteen community colleges throughout the state. In its formative years, the University was several times rescued by President James K. Patterson (right) who, at one time, pledged his own funds to finish construction of what is now the Administration Building.

Kentucky long made little or no provision for black students. But in 1886 the Legislature established Kentucky State College in Frankfort. The first building, below, was named for President John H. Jackson.

The all-male band (above) in 1893 reflected the predominance of men in the A & M College of Kentucky. Women were grudgingly admitted to the University after 1880.

The annual traditional flag rush, tugs-of-war, and the pranks of male students at Kentucky A & M (below) were sometimes rough.

Cadets at the A & M College of Kentucky (later University of Kentucky), established at Lexington in February, 1865, under the Morrill Land Grant Act, are shown above drilling in front of the Administration Building.

William Jennings Bryan, famous for his "Cross of Gold" speech on free silver and for his stand against evolution, is shown (below) seated in the car with H. S. Barker (in bowler hat), president of the University of Kentucky.

Within the first quarter of the twentieth century, the Commonwealth established four new teachers' colleges. In 1966 they were elevated to university status: Western Kentucky University (left) at Bowling Green; Eastern Kentucky at Richmond; Morehead State at Morehead; and Murray State at Murray.

Kentucky's libraries are concentrated in Lexington and Louisville.

The University of Kentucky's general library, in Lexington, has well over a million volumes and many microfilms and manuscripts.

Both the Lexington Public Library and the Louisville Free Public Library originated in the eighteenth century. George Washington, John Adams, and Aaron Burr are thought to have contributed to the infant "Transylvania Library," chartered in 1795—the beginning of the Lexington Public Library.

Noteworthy historical collections are maintained by the Filson Club in Louisville (left), one of America's greatest private historical societies, and the Kentucky Historical Society in Frankfort, one of the country's earliest state-supported historical societies.

The library of Transylvania University contains an outstanding collection of early medical books.

X. THE ARTS AND SCIENCES

JOHN JAMES AUDUBON is the most famous of the artists claimed by Kentucky. Many important paintings, which later appeared in his monumental *Birds of America,* were completed during his residence around Henderson from 1810 to 1819.

Preferring to study and portray birds, Audubon neglected his business affairs to travel about Kentucky, a paradise for naturalists with its varied and abundant plant and animal life. His observations of Kentuckians were recounted in his *Delineations of American Life.* A large collection of the prints from the elephant folio is in Audubon State Park near Henderson.

Audubon's group of birds on the opposite page includes the extinct Carolina parakeet and three flycatchers. His cardinal (Kentucky's state bird) is below.

Alexander Wilson, who came to America from Scotland about 1794, visited Kentucky where he met and influenced Audubon. Wilson had studied birds and was a self-taught artist (his red tanagers are below, right). The nine volumes of his *American Ornithology* were published from 1808 to 1814.

Portrait painters abounded in early nineteenth-century Kentucky, where newly affluent families were eager to have their likenesses preserved on canvas. Of these artists, Matthew Harris Jouett was by far the most successful. Born in Mercer County, Jouett (upper right) first studied law, like most bright young men of his time. But his real interest lay in drawing and painting. He was Gilbert Stuart's pupil in Boston and became the first prominent painter in the West.

In Kentucky he executed numerous portraits, including those of such notables as Isaac Shelby, Robert Letcher, Horace Holley, Robert S. Todd, Gideon Shryock, Asa Blanchard, Judge George M. Bibb, John Rowan, John C. Breckinridge, and Henry Clay.

Jouett was a prolific painter, and among his numerous portraits is a noteworthy one of Lafay-

ette in the Capitol in Frankfort and one of John Grimes, a pre-Civil War artist, in the Metropolitan Museum in New York.

A family portrait by one of the early artists is cherished by Kentuckians of today as a mark of distinction.

Among the antebellum painters who flourished in Kentucky were Joseph H. Bush (below), who as a portraitist ranked next to Jouett.

Thomas S. Noble (opposite page, lower left) was a post-Civil War painter who won national recognition.

Frank Duveneck, internationally famous portrait and genre painter as well as sculptor, was born in Covington. His "Cobbler's Apprentice" is at the upper right.

Joel T. Hart (below, right) once carved epitaphs on tombstones in a Lexington marble yard, but later studied sculpture and worked in Italy. His busts of Henry Clay and Andrew Jackson are among his best known works.

The prolific Paul Sawyier (1865-1917) expressed his love of the Kentucky River country in his oils and watercolors. His "Covered Bridge" and "Elkhorn Creek" are below. Sawyier also painted numerous scenes of old Frankfort.

The foremost Kentucky animal painter of the nineteenth century was Edward Troye (below, right). The Swiss-born artist was at his best in portraying American blooded horses and cattle. He died in Georgetown, July 25, 1874.

Constantine Samuel Rafinesque (above) taught natural history and botany at Transylvania University from 1819 to 1826. The evolutionary theories of the eccentric Rafinesque predated those of Charles Darwin.

In 1787 John Fitch (see plaque at right) successfully operated a steamboat on the Delaware River. Fitch, also an early silversmith in Kentucky, did not realize either fame or fortune from his invention.

John Filson, an early Lexington academy master, published his book *Kentucke* in 1784 (upper left, opposite page) with a map which appears on the endpapers of this volume.

Thomas Hunt Morgan (1866-1945) (opposite page, upper right), a native of Lexington, received the Nobel Prize in 1933 for his development of the gene theory of heredity. Morgan received the B.S. and M.S. degrees at the A&M College, where his French instructor was a former Union officer who had once been captured by his famous uncle.

Nathan Stubblefield, an inventor from Murray in Calloway County, is said to have been the first to build and demonstrate a "wireless telephone." He successfully demonstrated his invention in January 1902 before a group of scientists and newspapermen in Washington, D.C. The photograph at lower right was probably taken around 1902.

Thomas H. Barlow (1789-1865), native Lexingtonian built the first steam locomotive in the West for the Lexington & Ohio Railroad. In addition, he invented a planetarium, a rifled cannon, and a self-feeding nail and tack machine.

THE

DISCOVERY, SETTLEMENT

And present State of

KENTUCKE:

A N D

An ESSAY towards the TOPOGRAPHY, and NATURAL HISTORY of that important Country:

To which is added,

An A P P E N D I X,

C O N T A I N I N G,

I. The ADVENTURES of Col. *Daniel Boon*, one of the first Settlers, comprehending every important Occurrence in the political History of that Province.

II The MINUTES of the *Piankashaw* council, held at *Post St. Vincents, April* 15, 1784.

III. An ACCOUNT of the *Indian* Nations inhabiting within the Limits of the Thirteen United States, their Manners and Customs, and Reflections on their Origin.

IV. The STAGES and DISTANCES between *Philadelphia* and the Falls of the *Ohio;* from *Pittsburg* to *Pensacola* and several other Places. —The Whole illustrated by a new and accurate MAP of *Kentucke* and the Country adjoining, drawn from actual Surveys.

By *J O H N F I L S O N.*

Wilmington, Printed by JAMES ADAMS, 1784.

The theater of Louisville and Lexington early in the century was a stepping stone for many an aspiring actor and actress. Macauley's Theatre (above) in Louisville opened October 13, 1873.

Kentucky is known for its folk music, both traditional and popular. Francis James Child and John Jacob Niles have made known many of the English and Scottish ballads from eastern Kentucky. Colonel Nicholas "Sandy" Falkner of Scott County wrote "The Arkansas Traveler," a prototype of country music. The cover of the first edition of Stephen Foster's "My Old Kentucky Home," the state song, is at left.

Kentucky journalism has been shaped by the colorful personalities of such editors as Henry Watterson (left), of the *Louisville Courier-Journal*. From 1868 until his retirement in 1918, "Marse" Henry's spirited editorials focused public opinion upon the needs of the post-Civil War South. Although prosouthern in his sympathies, Watterson actively sought the reconciliation of his divided country. The *Courier-Journal* today, as in Watterson's time, ranks as one of the nation's best known newspapers.

John Bradford (below, left) and his brother Fielding used a small handpress for printing the *Kentucke Gazette* in Lexington. The first edition, on August 11, 1787, was late because most of the type, already set, had fallen into "pi" while being carried by pack horse from Limestone (Maysville) to Lexington. But the little *Gazette* was the first newspaper west of the Alleghenies and continued for many years.

As the Commonwealth became more settled, newspapers appeared in every county seat. Many were short-lived, others finally merged with competitors. Most allied themselves with political causes and waged vigorous, sometimes vitriolic, editorial war against their opposition.

The Louisville *Advertiser*, edited by Shadrach Penn, became Kentucky's first daily newspaper in 1826, eight years after its founding.

Kentucky literature has its roots in the eighteenth century. John Filson could be considered a Kentuckian, and David Rice wrote his antislavery tract in the year of Kentucky's statehood. Many early nineteenth-century works are of antiquarian interest only. Jesse Lynch Holman's *Prisoners of Niagara, or the Errors of Education* (1810), the first novel written by a native Kentuckian, was so poorly written that the author tried to destroy all copies, making his book an expensive rarity.

Not until after the Civil War did Kentucky literature emerge into the main stream of American letters. James Lane Allen (upper left), born in 1849 near Lexington, wrote novels in the "genteel" tradition, notably *A Kentucky Cardinal, Aftermath,* and *The Choir Invisible. The Reign of Law,* a story of the impact of science on a fundamentalist society, had an international influence.

John Fox, Jr. (left), sympathetically portrayed the mountaineers of eastern Kentucky in his stories and novels, the best known of which are *The Trail of the Lonesome Pine* and *The Little Shepherd of Kingdom Come.*

Madison Cawein (opposite page, near right), became one of America's best lyric poets. The gentle and sensitive Cawein, born in Louisville of poor parents in 1865, left school at an early age. A deep love of nature is reflected in his poems.

By the mid-twentieth century, Kentucky authors were making major literary contributions. Thomas Merton, Father Louis of the Cistercian, or Trappist Order, at Gethsemani in Nelson County, won acclaim as poet and essayist. Poet-novelist Robert Penn Warren (above) was one of the Fugitive group that developed the new criticism in the thirties. He won the Pulitzer Prize for *All the King's Men*, a novel based upon the rise and fall of Louisiana's Huey P. Long. Many of his other works draw on Kentucky traditions and events. Harriette Arnow, Janice Holt Giles and Elizabeth Madox Roberts are other noted Kentucky authors.

Dr. Willard R. Jillson (right) of Frankfort is former State Geologist and author of a number of books on Kentucky history and geology.

THE SKIPPER ALWAYS CARRIES A FOLDING PLAY-PEN
ON THE KINDERGARTEN SPECIAL

"HERE THEY IS, MIS' MARY! COME AND GIT 'EM!"

MISS MARY WORTLE'S KINDER GARTEN

F. FOX

Humorist Irvin S. Cobb (above), born in Paducah in 1876, became a noted New York journalist and columnist. He is best known for his stories of Kentucky local color, first collected in *Old Judge Priest*; other books are *Red Likker* and his autobiography, *Exit Laughing*.

Fontaine Talbot Fox, Jr., was cartoonist for Louisville newspapers and later for the Chicago *Evening Post*. After 1915 his cartoons were syndicated. His comic strip, *The Toonerville Trolley* (above), was inspired in part by the old Louisville trolley lines.

Prolific author Jesse Stuart (right) of Greenup County came to prominence in 1934 with the publication of his 700 sonnets in *Man with a Bull-Tongue Plow*. His essays, poetry, short stories, and novels since have been widely translated and used in anthologies throughout the world.

150

William H. Townsend (above), Lexington attorney who became a historian of distinction and famous as a raconteur, founded the Kentucky Civil War Round Table in 1953. His address on Cassius M. Clay, before the Chicago Civil War Round Table (1952), was a nationally distributed recording, and his recollections of life in Kentucky are preserved in the witty *Hundred Proof.* A Lincoln scholar, he wrote *Lincoln and the Bluegrass* and other books.

The library at Henry Clay's home, Ashland, makes an appropriate gathering place for these Kentucky historians who have achieved fame as scholars. On the front row, from left: Clement Eaton, Thomas D. Clark, and J. Winston Coleman, Jr. Back row, from left: Albert D. Kirwan, Holman Hamilton, and Hambleton Tapp. The portrait of Clay in the background is by Jouett.

Medicine

On the early nineteenth-century frontier, medical knowledge and facilities were scanty and crude. For isolated settlers, they were virtually nonexistent. The pioneer depended on home remedies, local traditions, and perhaps a book of folk medicine which described all manner of maladies with their proper cures.

Homemade prescriptions used recipes already ancient when immigrants brought them to America, as well as some learned from Indians. These concoctions were brewed from things such as white walnut bark, sassafras, dogwood, willow, catnip, pennyroyal, sulphur, eggs, and goose grease.

Most pioneers knew little about hygiene and sanitation. Infant and maternal death rates were high; ague was regarded as inescapable and the dreaded small pox, malaria, typhoid fever, and cholera took a fearful toll of lives.

The rapid growth of towns created problems equally as dangerous as those of the isolated hamlets.

Some doctors studied medicine by observing and assisting a practicing physician. But in the late eighteenth century, attempts were made to replace this old tutorial system with formal training. Young Americans studied at the celebrated medical centers in Paris and Edinburgh and in the schools which, as early as 1765, began to open in this country, notably in Philadelphia.

In 1799 Transylvania University in Lexington launched its medical department—the first in the West—with the appointment of Doctors Frederick Ridgely and Samuel Brown as professors of surgery. A brilliant faculty was recruited, and by the 1820s the Kentucky school rivaled that of Harvard.

Among the scholars and educators who contributed to Transylvania's growing reputation was Daniel Drake (right), who wrote *Pioneer Life in Kentucky* with as much authority as *The Principal Diseases of the Interior Valley of North America.*

Practicing under less than ideal conditions, Kentucky's pioneer physicians nevertheless made important contributions to medical progress. In the small settlement of Danville in December 1809, Doctor Ephriam McDowell (right) performed the first ovariotomy in medical history. The patient recovered and lived for over thirty years after the operation. An artist's conjectural view of the operation is on the opposite page. The McDowell home (below), on the second floor of which the operation took place, is preserved as a museum.

In 1806 Walter Brashear at Bardstown completed the first successful hip-joint amputation.

Other outstanding early doctors included Benjamin W. Dudley and his protégé, James M. Bush, both fine surgeons and lithotomists. Samuel Gross of Louisville published *A System of Surgery* (1859), one of the classics in the field.

Charles Wilkins Short was a pioneer in botany and its application to materia medica.

John Esten Cooke, an early member of the Transylvania faculty, saw the liver as responsible for most human ailments. His lavish use of calomel was notorious and later discredited.

In February 1816, the first mental asylum in the West, and the second in the United States, was established in Lexington.

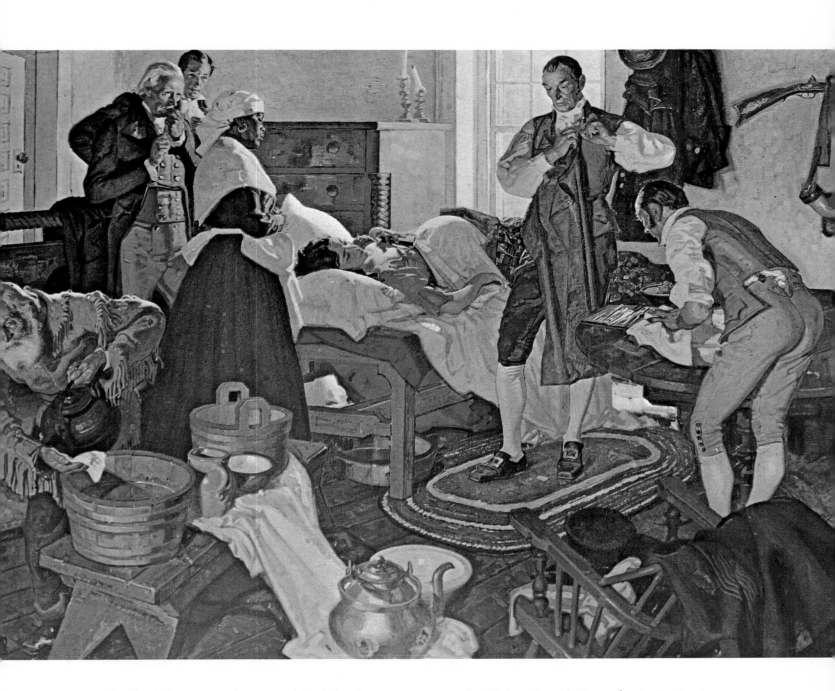

In 1837 half of the Transylvania medical faculty moved to Louisville to staff the Medical Institute, which later attracted such men as Drake, Gross, and Austin Flint. The Institute became in 1845 the Medical Department of the University of Louisville.

Postponed for many years, plans for a medical center at the University of Kentucky in Lexington received legislative approval in 1956. The A. B. Chandler Medical Center contains three colleges—Medicine, Dentistry, Nursing, and a school of Allied Health Professions as well as a 400-bed hospital.

Samuel Brown, Edinburgh-trained, was the founder of Transylvania's medical department. He established his reputation as a pioneer doctor by vaccinating some five hundred persons against smallpox by 1802. Physicians in New York and Philadelphia were just beginning to experiment with the process. Its discoverer, Edward Jenner, who published the results of his experiments in 1798, was still having difficulty convincing his English contemporaries of their value.

The medical department acquired an invaluable library and scientific apparatus from Europe, and by 1859 more than 6400 students had been enrolled there. A little more than 1850 doctors had been graduated to minister to the needs of the South and West when the department closed in 1859.

When cholera broke out in Lexington in 1833, everyone who could fled the town. William "King" Solomon, the town vagrant, however, became a hero when he stayed behind to dig graves and to bury the many victims of the plague. Solomon, whose services were once sold to an old Negro woman, "Aunt" Charlotte, is immortalized in James Lane Allen's *King Solomon of Kentucky*. His portrait at left is by General Samuel Woodson Price, Lexington artist.

The operation in 1809 to amputate George Rogers Clark's leg (below) was performed without anesthesia at his home near Louisville. So that neighbors would not hear his screams, Colonel George Rogers Clark Floyd, son of the General's closest friend, arranged for a fife and drum corps to play outside the window. The painting of the scene is by Ed Finch.

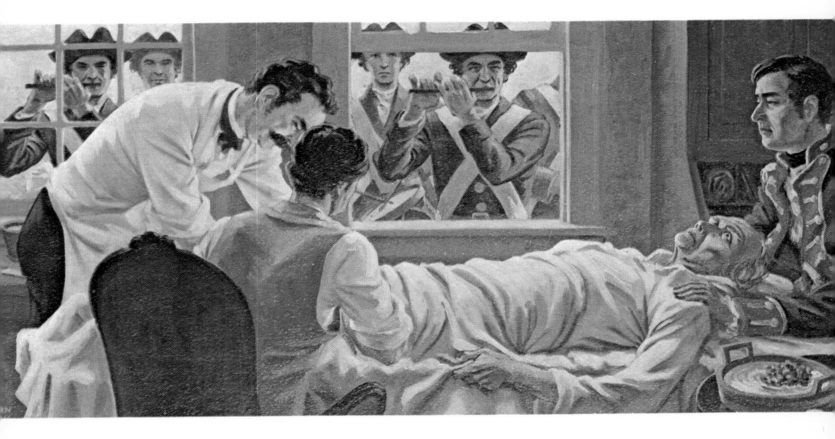

An old-time country doctor, such as W. E. Adams of Anderson County (above), might have a rather informal office. Doctor Adams's was in the side yard of his home. From the array of bottles on shelves and counters, he mixed his own prescriptions.

Often the rural doctor's patients would pay their bills with hams, calves, pigs, lambs, or plow gear.

The Frontier Nursing Service, founded in 1925 by Mary Breckinridge, maintains several centers (right) in isolated and almost inaccessible areas around Hyden in Leslie County. Each center has a clinic and living quarters for two nurse-midwives who are assigned to an area of some eighty square miles.

XI. CRAFTS

KENTUCKY craftsmanship was early displayed in the building and furnishing of the settler's home, when everything that was needed had to be made by hand. Even pottery and some glass and metal objects were produced by the family or by a skilled craftsman in some settlements.

But crafts were a social influence as well as an economic necessity. Some of the great occasions in the pioneer's life were quilting bees and house raisings. The quality of the coverlets ("kivers") a woman wove and the way a man built a fence helped determine the family's standing. Children were taught the traditional skills; quilt patterns and weaving drafts were traded in a community; articles were made for the old and needy—all as a part of daily life.

Much of the work of Kentucky artisans, like these quaint glass bottles, possessed both beauty and utility. This unusual stove was used by the Shakers at Pleasant Hill as an ingenious solution to the problem of heating a steady supply of "sad irons" on ironing day.

Some crafts, like blacksmithing and glassblowing, lent themselves to specialization. The trade from a community could support a blacksmith who fashioned metal goods such as the ox shoes at right. The cloven hoof required two shoes.

The old "fire dogs" (opposite page) were cast at the Churchill-Buckner furnace in Muhlenberg County in the 1830s. Also known as "dog irons," they were used in an open fireplace to prevent burning logs from rolling out onto the floor and setting the house afire.

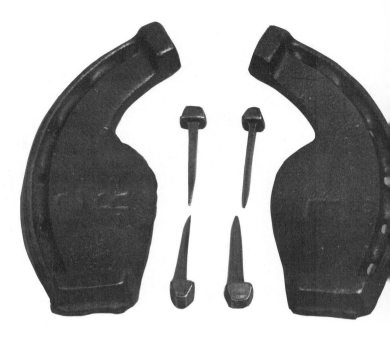

Woodworking, including cabinetry, furniture-making, carving and whittling, has been a traditional craft in the forested eastern mountains. Chairs like many found in Kentucky mountain homes are shown in two stages of production in the picture at far left (opposite page) and below left. The third craftsman (center) is constructing a loom.

By the end of the nineteenth century, industrialization in America had changed the old self-reliant manner of living. No longer did a family need to produce most of what its members ate, wore, or used. People could buy cheaply the articles they had once made with love and care.

Handweaving had died out in most cases by the end of the Civil War. Other crafts, even in the isolated eastern Kentucky mountains, were also disappearing.

But in the 1890s, the handiwork of the Appalachian highlanders was rediscovered by interested "outsiders," mostly northerners. The old skills were encouraged and taught again. The mountain people found their forefathers' crafts a source of a productive industry.

Available materials were used to create the necessities of everyday living. Corn shucks, for example, were used for everything from dolls to chair seats to horse collars. Brooms have been made from sedge, broomcorn, and even oak splits and twigs. Their production was updated a bit in the assembly line (right) in Carlisle County. The small decorative hearth brooms, which can be seen hanging from the rafters of the porch, are more often made for sale today.

The settlers' children were entertained by toys of such materials as corn shucks and stalks, cloth, straw, clay, and wood. Orlenia Ritchie, from Knott County (opposite page), holds a puppet she carved from wood.

"Gritting" corn into meal for bread (opposite page) and riving shingles for roofing (below, left) were once familiar tasks. Handmade musical instruments like the dulcimer (below), brought some beauty into the otherwise drab existence of the Kentucky highlander. John Jacob Niles (below, left), composer and collector of ballads, has encouraged a renewed interest in making these instruments.

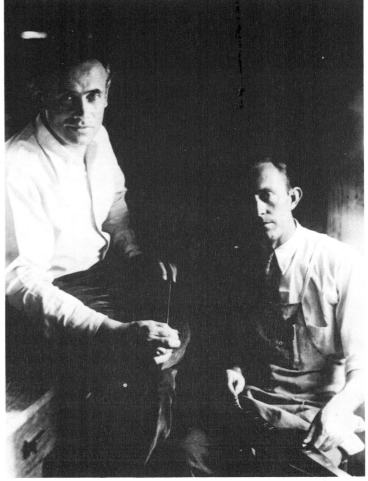

A pioneer girl's chances of making a good marriage were considerably enhanced if she was skilled in the use of the spinning wheel, loom, and needle. Woven "kiverlids," or coverlets, like those at left beautified simple homes.

The early Kentucky coffin quilt (opposite page) has a border of caskets stitched with the names of family members. As each person died, his casket was permanently moved to the "cemetery" in the center of the quilt.

A lively and imaginative use of appliqué, paint, and embroidery produced this interesting friendship quilt (above). Birds, animals, flowers, and a fan are among the figures used to decorate this century-old quilt, the colorful patches of which were furnished by friends and neighbors.

The pioneer who fashioned furniture for his house, farm tools for himself, and perhaps shoes for the family probably never thought of himself as a craftsman. He was self-sufficient because he had to be to survive in a primitive society. He also had the reward of personal achievement for his efforts. If a man's handiwork was good enough for others to seek him out, he had more reason to be proud. The stone cutter below shaped tombstones for many family cemeteries in rural Breathitt County.

For girls and women appliquéing a quilt such as the "Tree of Life" quilt at the right (above) or creating a delicate needlepoint sampler (opposite page) were practical as well as decorative skills.

The old ways persisted longest in the southern Appalachians, which include much of eastern Kentucky, mainly because of financial need. People in the mountains were still using handmade and handwoven items even as industrial progress elsewhere eliminated the need for much hand labor.

Since the old crafts had not entirely died out, there was a basis for their revival. Many mountain women, around the turn of the century, dusted off antique spinning wheels or looms that had long stood in attics, and began adding to the family income.

Berea in Madison County became the stronghold of craftwork. Here students of poor mountain families bartered handmade items for "book learning"—the beginning of the famous Fireside Industries at Berea College.

Efforts are being made now to preserve such arts as basketweaving (above) by guilds and craft centers which help individual craftsmen with design, production, and marketing.

In Kentucky today, traditional, contemporary, and experimental crafts may all be found coexisting harmoniously.

Silversmiths

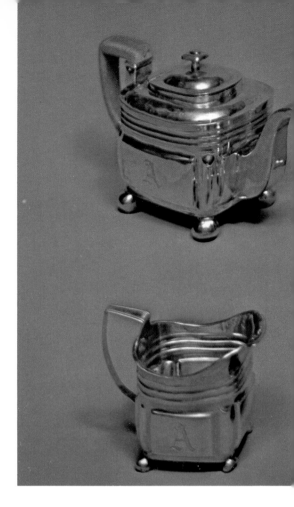

As EARLY as 1785 Joshua Humphreys and Edward West were busy in their shops in Lexington. Not long afterward they were joined by others in such towns as Paris, Bardstown, and Louisville. The growing affluence among Kentuckians and the popularity of silver pieces as prizes at fairs and races gave Kentucky's silversmiths ample opportunity to exercise their craft. From the 1820s through the Civil War silvermaking flourished in Kentucky, and Lexington, the "Athens of the West," became noted for the elegance of its ware.

The source of the metal used by these smiths was silver coinage, hence the name "coin silver" that is applied to their work. Usually the head of a household would visit the smith's shop carrying his accumulated coins, a list of the articles desired, and a rough sketch of the pattern or design. The tea service, christening bowl, and mug (left) by Asa Blanchard, most famous of Kentucky's silversmiths, may have been created in just such a way.

The coin silver ladles (lower left, opposite page) are representatives of the work of the early silversmiths. The daily ledger beside them chronicled the transactions of T. K. Marsh, a silversmith in Paris, Bourbon County.

The pitchers and cups at left represent a grouping of the work of Blanchard, Eli Garner, Poindexter, and John Kitts. Like the mint julep cups below, they were once offered as prizes in livestock competitions and horse races.

John Fitch, one of the earliest Kentucky silversmiths, had twenty apprentices in New Jersey before he moved to the West. An experimenter, Fitch is credited with having devised the first American steamboat.

A tradition was born when nine silver cups were offered as premiums at the first "Shew and Cattle Fair," July 25, 1816, at the Lewis Sanders farm on the Georgetown Pike near Lexington in Fayette County.

Cabinetmaking

Even before Kentucky became a state, there were several cabinetmakers turning out sturdy furniture to be used in the log cabins and houses of the settlements. They made almost everything that was needed—from spinning wheels to cupboards to horse-drawn wagons. Later, as the Indian menace abated, they fashioned fine furniture and woodwork for plantation homes and for the brick houses and the shops of a dozen Kentucky towns.

Nearly all of these early cabinetmakers in the Commonwealth came from Virginia, Pennsylvania, and Maryland. At first they used native walnut, maple, and wild cherry; later they imported mahogany to create some of the fine pieces that are treasured as antiques in Kentucky homes today.

At least forty-five cabinet-makers were working in Kentucky when it joined the Union in 1792. Their apprentices, risen to the level of journeymen, traveled all over the state to make furniture and wall cabinets for courthouses, taverns, churches, and homes.

The early Sheraton table (opposite page) was made about 1815. The Chippendale secretary (1796) has secret drawers. William Fulton made the walnut sewing table and chair (above) in Louisville in 1837. The Empire-style bureau (left) was a product of Ward & Stokes in Louisville (1840s). Porter Clay, brother of Henry, was an early Lexington cabinetmaker.

XII. THE PEOPLE

KENTUCKY, the original gateway to the West, has seen the ebb and flow of the varied tides of American life. Its people have moved in from the eastern seaboard and outward to the South, the West, and the Midwest.

In the mountains, for so long remote and inaccessible, the ways and customs of the Scotch-Irish pioneers survived into the twentieth century. In the Bluegrass can be found the settled charm of the Old Dominion. Small farmers dominate the south-central region—independent, close to the land and its weathers. The Purchase with its level fields dreaming under the summer sun is an en-

clave of the Deep South. Along the Ohio there is the bustle and busyness of the Middle West. All of these strands have been woven into the rich diversity of Kentucky's life and people, its folkways and customs—barbecues, court days, weddings, and funerals.

The main street of Paris about 1810 (below) reflects the rural flavor of early days in the Bluegrass. The small bucket (below, right) carried live coals from one household to another at a time when matches were not common; the other utensil is a pioneer lamp.

B J CLAY.   GEN L. WOOL.   GEN. WINFIELD SCOTT.   J. DUNCAN.   M. HURLER.   MR DAVIS.
Candidate for President.   HULCHCRAFT.   S. BROOKS

BOURBON FAIR, KY. 1852.

The Bourbon County Fair scene (above) with its background of ladies in bonnets was dignified by the presence of General Winfield Scott (next to the steps) when he was a candidate for president in 1852. A madstone (below, right) was highly regarded by the early settlers as a cure for hydrophobia. The stone was soaked in milk and applied to a wound; if it did not adhere, the victim was thought to be free of rabies. Kit Carson's birthplace in Madison County illustrates Kentucky's ties with the West.

Held once a month on the public square of the county seat, court day attracted people from miles around.

On Cheapside in Lexington (above and at right), social distinctions were forgotten as people examined the motley assortment of livestock and discussed crops, weather, and politics. Lining the courthouse yard were such items as homemade baskets and chairs, old clothing, furniture, buggy harness and plow gear, and sorghum cane "sweetening." Everything was for sale, or trade.

Court day in Lexington was declared a public nuisance and officially banned in 1921.

"County Court Day", Lexington, Ky.

174

Public Square, on Court Day, Mt. Sterling, Ky.

Lotteries were the favorite means of raising money for schools, libraries, colleges, Masonic lodges, courthouses and other civic improvements. Generous prizes were awarded to the holders of lucky tickets in the 1863 Shelby College lottery in Covington.

The holiday atmosphere of an old-fashioned court day is recreated once a year in Mount Sterling, seat of Montgomery County.

The merchandise offered is as varied as ever: coon dogs, antique whiskey bottles, gallons of sorghum molasses, guns, knives, and furniture. A sharp trade at court day is as satisfying now as it was in less sophisticated times.

Social gatherings of every sort appealed to gregarious Kentuckians. The monotony of pioneer life was relieved by picnics, barbecues, militia musters, speakings, and sporting contests. Barn and house "raisings" involved heavy labor, but they offered social relaxation too.

A wedding, perhaps, was taking place in the old Phoenix Hotel on Lexington's Main Street (upper right) about 1861-1863. Formerly Postlethwait's Tavern, the hotel (center of the photograph) has operated on this corner since the mid-1790s. The two-horse omnibus in front of the Phoenix met trains at the station and carried travelers to their hotels.

County fairs, like court days, were major events for country and townspeople alike. The one held each year since 1854 at Germantown in Bracken County is the oldest continuing fair in Kentucky. The photograph at right (early 1900s) shows the two-story wooden amphitheater for spectators. From the height of the judges' stand, reached by a ladder, fine cattle, horses, mules, and other livestock have been viewed for over a century.

The scene (lower right) on the midway of the Kentucky State Fair indicates the current popularity of this form of entertainment.

EXCURSION!

on the Steamer

→ MAGGIE HARPER, ←

TO

LOISVILLE,

SATURDAY, MAY 17th, '84

The best of order. Seats for everybody. Prof. Hollis' Orchestra, assisted by Will Wright. No Liquors sold on the boat. This will be the Boss Excursion of them all.

Look at the List of attractions in Louisville on the 17th.

You Can't Afford to Miss it.

McCauley's Theatre--Clara Morris in New Magdaline and Article 47. Whalen's Theatre, American Flats. Louisville Jocky Club, Spring Meeting; 5 races Saturday, 44 entries first race at 2.30. Base Ball Park, game called at 2.30.

The Boat will leave Louisville at 12 o'clock at night. giving those who attend the races and base ball game an opportunity to go to the Theatre at night.

LEAVES CARROLLTON at 5.30 o'clock
" MADISON, " 7 o'clock

IT'S A GO, RAIN OR SHINE.

Fare, Adults, Round Trip 75 Cts.
Fare, Children, Round Trip 25 cts.

Staterooms $1,00 additional. Telephone Capt. Andy Henry at the Wharf boat if you want one.

Remember the day May 17,

SAM. S. FEARN, Master.

N. B. NEXT EXCURSION, MAY, 24.

Excursions by river steamers such as the *Maggie Harper* brought many rural and small-town Kentuckians to Louisville and Cincinnati to sample the diversions of the city. The trip itself, enlivened by music from an orchestra, promised to be festive.

The outing pictured below, probably a school, church, or Sunday school picnic, was held in the early 1900s. The barge, pushed by a steamboat, had a coal oil lamp on its top deck and could be used for nighttime expeditions.

Around the turn of the century, only Louisville among Kentucky towns had a population of more than 50,000. Most Kentuckians traded, exchanged gossip, sought legal advice and medical care in county seats such as Whitesburg (below), in Letcher County. The courthouse with its tower is at the right side of the muddy, unpaved main street of this typical eastern Kentucky community.

Eminence in Henry County (above) had the advantage of being on a branch railroad line. Incorporated in 1851, the town was a thriving trade center for the surrounding rural area.

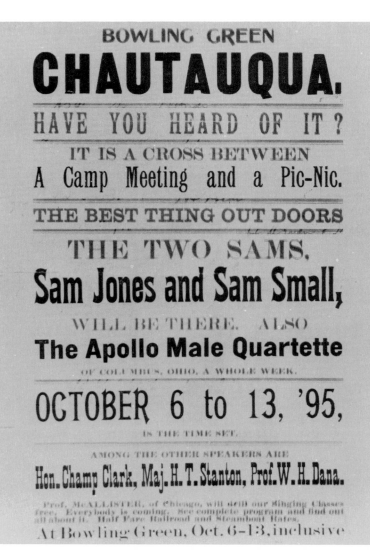

BOWLING GREEN

CHAUTAUQUA.

HAVE YOU HEARD OF IT ?

IT IS A CROSS BETWEEN

A Camp Meeting and a Pic-Nic.

THE BEST THING OUT DOORS

THE TWO SAMS,

Sam Jones and Sam Small,

WILL BE THERE. ALSO

The Apollo Male Quartette

OF COLUMBUS, OHIO, A WHOLE WEEK.

OCTOBER 6 to 13, '95,

IS THE TIME SET.

AMONG THE OTHER SPEAKERS ARE

Hon. Champ Clark, Maj. H. T. Stanton, Prof. W. H. Dana.

Prof. McALLISTER, of Chicago, will drill our Singing Classes
free. Everybody is coming. See complete program and find out
all about it. Half Fare Railroad and Steamboat Rates.

At Bowling Green, Oct. 6-13, inclusive

The Redpath Chautauqua Special (above), en route from Chicago to the South in 1913, is greeted at a railway station in a Kentucky town. The Chautauqua was a principal source of cultural improvement and entertainment in Kentucky, as in other states at this period. The movement took its name from the institution at Chautauqua, New York, established in 1874; originating as an extension of the summer Sunday school, it offered an eight-week course in arts, science, and humanities. Chautauqua became a commercial enterprise in 1912.

The photographs on this page (and many in the crafts section) are from the excellent Doris Ulmann collection at Berea College. Miss Ulmann recorded with her camera the disappearing folkways of the eastern Kentucky mountain people during the 1920s.

At right, wool is soaked in an iron pot of dye (which was usually homemade) before being hung up to dry. Early Kentucky wool coverlets, or "kivers," were made of this home-dyed wool.

The girl (at right) is spinning flax, which was used to make fine linen, handkerchiefs, and tablecloths.

This mountain home in eastern Kentucky is covered with handmade "shakes," or shingles, and the cracks in the log walls are filled with stones and mud to keep out the cold. The head of the household displays his worldly possessions: a single-barrel shotgun, a banjo, a revolver, and a copy of *Crittenden*, by John Fox, Jr.

The old mountaineer at left is shown about 1890-1895 with his Kentucky "ground wagon," a homemade sled used for hauling small loads and farm produce.

The small mountain cabin above sheltered a large family beneath its "shake" roof.

Rural free delivery did not appeal to many rural Kentuckians as much as a visit to a country post office in crossroads establishments like the Rock House Store (below) in Letcher County. The storekeeper-postmaster with his federal appointment was an important man in the community. He also knew more about what went on locally than almost anyone else; not only was his store a center of trade, but of neighborhood gossip and news as well.

A farmer and his family had just arrived to shop in the typical country town of Woodbury, Butler County, when this picture was taken about 1900.

The owner of this mountain home (middle left) near Slade, in Powell County, poses at the split hickory fence.

The view at left is of a mountain community on the Cumberland River in Bell County in the early years of this century.

The skins of several kinds of animals, drying and ready for market, are stretched on the walls of this cabin in the eastern Kentucky mountains.

No political rally, patriotic gathering, or horse race was complete without its burgoo feast, served in tin cups. Burgoo, strictly a Kentucky dish, is properly cooked only in iron kettles out in the open as it was at this gathering about 1900 (top of page).

At barbecues like the one above, the meat was turned on spits over coals in long trenches as the cooking progressed.

Martin Van Buren Bates, shown above with his wife and a friend, was born in Letcher County in 1837. He eventually reached a height of seven feet and eleven inches, and weighed 525 pounds. After serving in the Confederate Army, he joined a circus and while touring Nova Scotia met Anna Swan, who was eight feet tall. The couple were later married in England, where they were introduced to Queen Victoria. Bates and his wife retired to Seville, Ohio, to a home built especially for them.

Jim Porter, the "Kentucky giant," was seven feet nine and one-half inches tall. He lived in Louisville during the years 1810-1859.

185

The dramatic effort to rescue Floyd Collins, trapped in Sand Cave near Cave City, was one of the most widely reported news stories between the two World Wars and became the subject of a popular Kentucky ballad. Collins, a commercial cave developer who owned nearby Crystal Cave, was exploring for new caves in February 1925 when a rock fell on his leg and pinned him in a passageway that would-be rescuers were unable to reach. For seventeen days Collins lay trapped, while rescue workers drilled a sixty-foot shaft from the surface—but when they reached him, he was dead. Collins's boots and the rock that imprisoned him are shown above.

*The Funeral Services of
Alice Merideth Peter
will take place at the residence of
her father, Prof. Robert Peter, on
the Newtown Turnpike road
(thence to Lexington Cemetery)
to-morrow, (Wednesday) afternoon
at 2 o'clock.*

Lexington, Ky., April 16, 1878.

Funeral customs of English origin were adapted to conditions in different parts of Kentucky. The little procession above was photographed in Harlan County in the early 1890s.

Funeral invitations were used to notify friends and neighbors when a death occurred and a service was scheduled before the weekly newspaper came out. A family servant distributed invitations to friends in the neighborhood, some were tacked up on posts in towns and villages, and others were placed in a bowl in the parlor of the deceased's home.

A happier scene is this rustic Harlan County wedding in 1893. The bridal altar has been raised under a buckeye, or horse-chestnut tree.

The Indian "medicine man" (upper left) is typical of those who hawked "cure-alls" at county court days in Kentucky. This man is crying his wares before a crowd on the public square at Morehead, Rowan County seat.

In the mountains and some other sections of the state, houses were built to protect the graves from rain. Often these structures contain metal and glass display cases with pictures of the deceased and, in the case of a child, a box with his playthings. The photograph shows a single and two double grave houses in an old churchyard at Sunnybrook in Wayne County.

188

The strange monument (above, center) in the cemetery at Mayfield, Graves County, was commissioned by Henry C. Wooldridge, a horse trader who died in 1899. The figures represent Wooldridge, his family, and his favorite animals. Most are by the Paducah sculptor, William Lydon.

Curious youngsters gather around a pond to watch a baptism by immersion. The little country church is nearby.

The study at left of a pensive mountain preacher is from the Doris Ulmann collection at Berea College.

The banjo player above represents an attempt to recapture the flavor of life in the time of Stephen Foster at Federal Hill in Bardstown.

In the early 1900s, there was time to enjoy life, and plenty of fish to be caught in Elkhorn Creek in the Bluegrass (above, right).

Mrs. Emma C. Clement, granddaughter of a slave, was named Mother of the Year in 1946, the first Negro woman so honored. A graduate of Livingstone College in North Carolina, she was married to George C. Clement, Bishop of the African Methodist Episcopal Zion Church. One of their seven children was Rufus E. Clement, a former president of Atlanta University.

The lot of the Negro improved little during the several decades following emancipation. Homes and living conditions remained at a level of squalor, and the cabin and family in Glasgow (above) were typical of the post-Civil War period.

Whitney Young, Jr., was director of the National Urban League from 1961 until his death in 1971. He was born in Lincoln Ridge in 1922 while his father was president of Lincoln Institute in Shelby County. Young, a graduate of Kentucky State College at Frankfort and of the University of Minnesota, served on seven presidential commissions and received the Medal of Freedom for his efforts to secure equal opportunity for black Americans. He was the author of *To Be Equal* and *Beyond Racism*.

Jean Thomas, the "Traipsin' Woman," earned that sobriquet when as a court reporter some years ago, she "traipsed," or traveled, from court to court on the circuit. Each year the American Folk Song Festival is held at the home of Miss Thomas near Ashland, where old-time mountain fiddlers like James Duff (left)—and some younger ones—vie with one another.

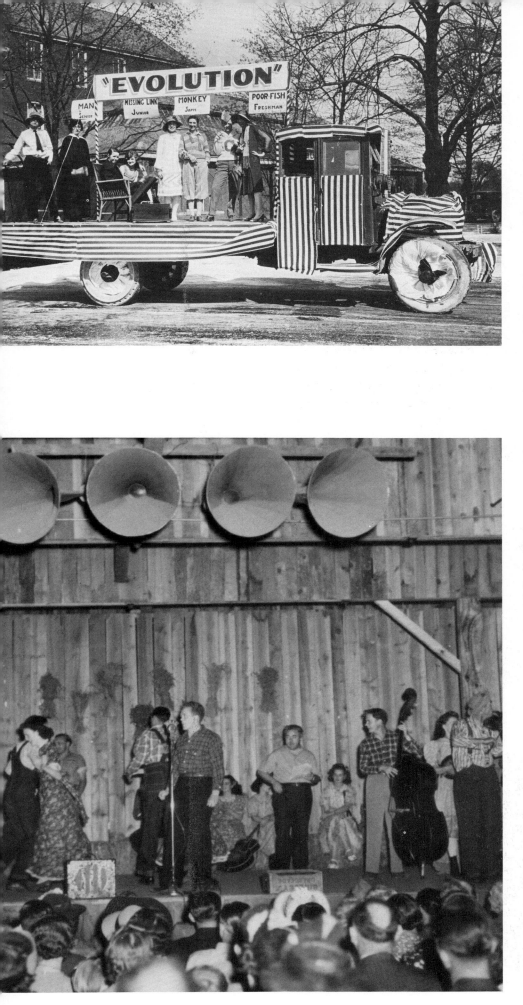

University of Kentucky students presented their version of evolution in this May Day float in the mid-1920s.

John T. Scopes, a member of the class of 1924, was the defendant in the famous "monkey trial" in Dayton, Tennessee, where he had been charged with teaching Charles Darwin's evolutionary theories in the local high school. Such teachings at the time were banned by state statute.

The issue was debated in the 1925 trial by two of the most noted lawyers of the time: Clarence Darrow, representing Scopes, and William Jennings Bryan for the prosecution.

The Renfro Valley Barn Dance has provided old fashioned entertainment on Saturday nights for many years. Local performers dance, sing, and play in a specially built barn about four miles west of Mount Vernon in Rockcastle County.

Livery stables like this one at Cynthiana, Harrison County seat, were local institutions as well as businesses until the mid-twenties. Here country people "put up" their rigs, surreys, and buggies when they arrived in town. This photograph was taken around 1900, some two decades before the coming of the automobile forced these stables out of business. Many of the buildings were then converted to other uses.

"Hoss" trading is a monthly event on Jockey Row near the Estill County courthouse at Irvine. Local and county men gather here to swap and buy horses, some of which are brokendown nags, others of fairly good pedigree.

The man examining the horse's teeth is about to make a trade. Something extra, "boot," was given when a good horse was exchanged for a poorer one. Traders claim that a horse's age up to nine years can be determined by the way his teeth are worn off. After that point, the age is anybody's guess.

Like horse trading, some things remain of earlier Kentucky life. A man who likes to hunt can find deer, wild turkey, quail, rabbit, squirrel, waterfowl, and coon—perhaps with hounds he acquired in an old-fashioned court day trade or bred on the farm.

Bourbon and Moonshine

In 1796, a part of the cargo of Colonel James Hillman, an experienced trader of the Ohio, consisted of whiskey which was sold to the Indians at $1.00 a quart, in the currency of the country, a deer skin being legal tender for a dollar and a doe skin half a dollar.
From Gould's
History of River Navigation.

Bᴙ ᴘᴀᴄᴋ ʜᴏʀsᴇ and flatboat, pioneers brought whiskey stills into Kentucky. They were sending barrels of whiskey out to market in the same manner before the eighteenth century had ended. For many early settlers, including Isaac Shelby, distilling was a relatively easy way to dispose of hard-to-ship grain.

Overland transportation at this period was inadequate, although Kentucky had numerous rivers and streams that emptied into the Ohio and Mississippi. Whiskey from the interior could be floated down to New Orleans. And at frontier military posts there was a heavy demand for the Indian trade, for a medium of exchange, and for "medical purposes."

The photograph (below, left) shows the office of Brown-Forman in Louisville about 1890 or 1900. The old gentleman seated at the desk on the far right is George Garvin Brown, founder of the company.

The name of the local product was derived from Bourbon County, which once included a large section of present-day Kentucky. Whiskey made in this huge area was called Bourbon, or Bourbon whiskey, a title that was becoming widely known by the time of the Civil War.

Also nationally prominent— in temperance reform—was Carrie Nation, a Garrard County native who set out to destroy saloons with her hatchet. The saloons, however, survived her "hatchetations" as well as her later antiliquor lectures. A bottle was named for her; it contained vinegar.

On the opposite page, a woman of the early 1900s grinds corn for the family still. Distilling was unlawful from the beginning of the Commonwealth unless one paid taxes.

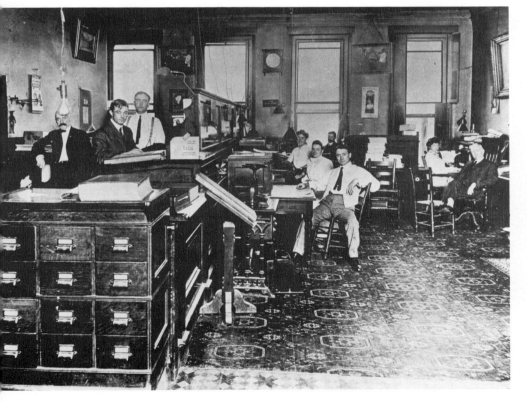

197

The free manufacture of corn whiskey, regarded as his right by many an independent Kentuckian, has been illegal from the earliest U.S. tax laws. Moonshine stills, like the one below, continued to operate in secluded areas despite the possibility of raids by "revenooers" (U.S. Treasury agents). One step in the distilling process involved heating the mash in the "cooker" (above).

During Prohibition, the town of Golden Pond in western Kentucky became famous as a moonshine center of America. Its "white lightning" went to the cities of the Midwest, distributed in part by the Al Capone gang of Chicago.

Strict supervision by the federal government as well as by corporate management is the principal difference between today's distilling industry and that of earlier times. The original Old Fitzgerald Distillery near Frankfort (above) was established in 1870. The small building at left was the first government bonded warehouse for bottling bonded whiskey, approved by Act of Congress, March 3, 1897. No automation was involved in getting barrels up the ramp into the warehouse.

Government regulations also required the licensing of liquor retailers. The Internal Revenue permit below was issued in the 1890s to Belle Breezing, a well-known Lexington "Madam" who maintained a "genteel house" on Megowan Street. She was said to have been the prototype for Belle Watling in *Gone with the Wind*.

Commemorative bottles like the one shown (above left) were issued by the Beam Distilling Company on the occasion of Kentucky's 175th anniversary in 1967.

The small settlement of Gethsemane was chosen for the location of Yellowstone Distillery in 1865 because the area abounded in good quality corn and limestone water. The warehouse is in the background (above).

Congress had repealed the National Prohibition Act the day before the photograph at left was made on December 6, 1933, at the Stitzel Distillery (now Stitzel-Weller) in Louisville.

In his twenty-eight years as a federal or revenue agent, William B. "Big Six" Henderson raided over five thousand stills and arrested some six thousand moonshiners in Kentucky. Henderson could call most of the moonshiners by their first names. The Commonwealth had ranked prominently among the moonshining states, but through efforts of federal agents such as Henderson, in recent years moonshining dropped considerably. In the photograph at right (opposite page), the legendary Henderson stands behind a confiscated still that has cooked its last gallon of mash.

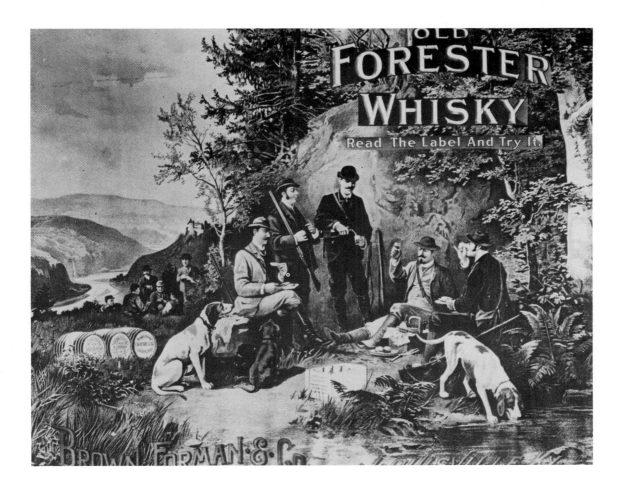

I want to git back —
    To the oldtime hills,
Whar the corn-juice runs
    Frum the old distills.
I want to git back —
    Yes, the good Lord knows,
I want to git back
    Whar the bluegrass grows,
        Back in old Kentucky.

JAMES TANDY ELLIS.

XIII. VIOLENCE

Indian tribes competing for hunting areas made a battleground of Kentucky even before the white man's attempts at settlement. Once the pioneers arrived, they became the targets of vengeful Indian attacks that often wiped out whole families. From the "half horse, half alligator" Indian fighter on the rampaging frontier there emerged Kentucky's tradition of violence.

A more recent symbol of violence is the mask (below) worn by a "night rider" during the dark tobacco planters' revolt in western Kentucky. On December 9, 1907, an armed and masked band of night riders destroyed $200,000 worth of property in Hopkinsville. The raiders terrorized the region in their attempts to check the power of several national tobacco companies that controlled the markets. Warehouses were burned and crops destroyed until the disturbance was quelled by state troops.

On several occasions mobs have lynched persons accused of crimes. While being taken to jail, William Barker killed the Lexington city marshal, July 10, 1858. Soon an infuriated crowd rushed Barker from the jail to the Fayette County Courthouse (below) where they hanged him from the second-story window.

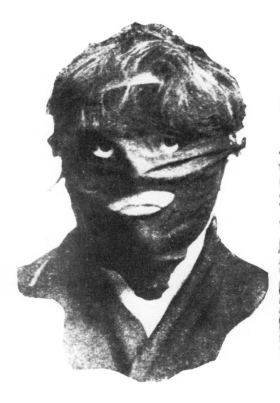

The conjectural drawing at left portrays the killing of Solomon P. Sharp by Jereboam O. Beauchamp on November 7, 1825, in Frankfort. Beauchamp, a young man from Simpson County, claimed that his wife, Ann Cook, had been seduced by Sharp who was then attorney general of Kentucky. While in jail, Beauchamp entered into a double suicide plot with his wife. She died, but Beauchamp lived long enough to be publicly hanged in the city where his crime was committed.

The couple were buried in a single grave in Bloomfield under a marker with an inscription romantic enough to assure a continued interest in the tragedy. The affair became the subject of several novels, including Robert Penn Warren's *World Enough and Time*.

Confederate guerrilla Champ Ferguson, shown at left with a guard, was accused at his trial in Nashville of having killed fifty-three persons. Many other victims were not mentioned in the charges. He was hanged October 20, 1865.

Angry mobs destroyed two antislavery newspaper offices —Cassius Clay's *The True American* in Lexington (August 18, 1845) and *The True South* in Newport (October 28–29, 1859).

From hatred engendered during the Civil War a number of feuds erupted in the Kentucky mountains. The most famous was the bloody vendetta between the Hatfields and the McCoys along the Kentucky–West Virginia border.

How long the ill-feeling had existed before the actual fighting began across the Tug River is uncertain. In 1880 an argument over the ownership of a lean razorback hog led into court. The Hatfields won the decision. Shortly afterwards a Hatfield was bushwhacked by a band said to be McCoys. Before the resulting feud had concluded with the battle of Grapevine Creek, some forty to fifty people had perished, including some that had simply "disappeared" in the mountains.

Anderson ("Devil Anse") Hatfield (above, left), the family leader, died a respected farmer in West Virginia in 1921. The photograph of the Hatfields (above) was taken during their feuding days. Two more feudists are shown at left.

An early feud was that between the Hill and Evans families in Garrard County. The feud began in 1840 over the return of a hired female slave and lasted for ten or twelve years. It was heightened by professional jealousy between Dr. O. P. Hill and Dr. Hezekial Evans.

GAME

To the Last, Poor Goebel

Is Fighting Death as He Fought His
Merciless Enemies.

"I'm Going To Live," He Whispers, Though
His Lips Are Growing Cold.

Before This Morning's Dawn the Victim of
a Hideous Plot Is Expected To Die,

The Bullets of the Cowardly Assassins Came From
Governor Taylor's Executive Building—
Thrilling Story of the Tragedy and
the Scenes That Followed.

REWARD

Awaits the Dying Leader,

Can He But Survive a Few Hours
For Its Confirmation.

Contest Committee Decided in Favor of
Democratic Standard Bearer,

And Eager Legislators Sought a Night Ses-
sion To Confer the Governorship

Before Death Could Claim the Stricken Man—
This Could Not Be Done, as Several Law-
makers Were Absent—Action To Be
Taken Early To-Day.

Governor-elect William Goebel (above, left) was killed by an unknown assassin on January 31, 1900. Goebel, a Democrat, was walking in front of the old State Capitol in Frankfort (below) when the fatal shot was fired from a second-story window of the State House next to the Capitol.

Several companies of the State Guard were brought to Frankfort to preserve order during the excitement that followed. Goebel died four days afterward. The identity of his assassin has never been definitely determined.

In 1908 racial unrest troubled the community of Olmstead in Logan County. Four Negroes, thought to be ringleaders were arrested on minor charges and confined in the Russellville jail. On the night of July 23, a lynch mob hanged them from this cedar tree just south of Russellville.

The crowd below rushed State Guards at the courthouse in Lexington on February 9, 1920, in an unsuccessful attempt to lynch Will Lockett, on trial for the murder of a ten-year-old girl. Six men died and fifty-odd were wounded in the shooting and martial law was proclaimed the same day.

Strong feeling against Catholics and Germans in Louisville prompted a general riot on election day, August 6, 1855, known as "Bloody Monday." About twenty-two people died as the result of the activities of the "Know-Nothing" party.

Jesse James and his gang robbed the Southern Bank of Kentucky (below) in Russellville on March 21, 1868. They relieved the bank of $14,000 but missed $50,000 because they did not stop to examine the vault. Afterwards the James boys hid out in Tennessee assuming the guise of farmers. They later held up the Deposit Bank at Columbia and the Cave City–Mammoth Cave stagecoach. Their activities from Kentucky to Kansas and as far north as Minnesota made them the most feared outlaws in the country.

When Ed Harris was tried on February 2, 1926, for the murder of three members of the Clarence Bryant family, Lexington was put under military rule with 1000 National Guardsmen stationed there. Harris was convicted. His was the last legal hanging (above) in Fayette County.

XIV. TWO WORLD WARS

FROM ALL OVER the Commonwealth, young men and women temporarily exchanged civilian status for a military life to serve their country in two global conflicts. Other Kentuckians worked on farms and in defense plants to help the war effort.

The *Kentucky*, shown below at its launching in 1898, was used as a training ship for recruits in 1917-1918. The battleship had previously served several years as flagship of the Southern Squadron in the Far East and was one of sixteen vessels which President Theodore Roosevelt sent on a round-the-world good will cruise in 1907-1909.

Distinguished Kentucky officers of World War I included, from left (top of opposite page), Major General George Brand Duncan; Colonel Charles D. Young; and Brigadier General Roger D. Williams.

General Duncan, an 1886 West Point graduate, commanded the 77th and 82nd Divisions during the war. He retired in 1925 and died in Lexington in 1950. Colonel Young was the highest ranking Negro army officer in World War I. Retired from the army for health reasons, Young rode his horse from Wilberforce University to Washington, D.C. He was afterwards reinstated and promoted to colonel. While representing this country as military attaché in Liberia, Colonel Young died of tropical fever in 1922. General Williams, who served in General George Custer's Sioux Indian campaign of 1876, was appointed commander of the 76th Brigade at Camp Shelby, Mississippi, in 1917. He was attached to the First Army headquarters in France from July 1918 to March 1919.

A Kentuckian, Victor Strahm (right) was an ace in World War I. From 1930 to 1942 he was chief of staff, Ninth U.S. Air Force, retiring in 1942 with the rank of brigadier general.

The almost-deserted appearance of Camp Taylor (lower right) near Louisville in 1917 was replaced by activity as recruits began training (opposite page), though there was still enough time, apparently, to tend lawn and flower plots (below).

After Pearl Harbor was attacked on December 7, 1941, Kentuckians served in all theaters of operation. Of the nearly 324,000 men and women in uniform by the end of the war, 4064 were killed in action and 6802 died in service.

Lieutenant General Simon Bolivar Buckner, Jr. (below), was the highest ranking United States officer killed in World War II. The son of a governor of Kentucky, he died in action on Okinawa on June 18, 1945. His body was returned and buried in the Frankfort cemetery on February 9, 1949.

The military became a temporary way of life for many young Kentuckians. Troops at right drill at Fort Knox in 1942. World War II troops wait in line at Camp Breckinridge near Morganfield in Union County in the 1940s.

XV. SPORTS

Almost as soon as they had made the first clearings in the forest, Kentuckians were indulging their fondness for horse racing, rifle shoots, foot races, wrestling, and bareknuckle fistfights. One of them, champion braggart and "king of the keel boaters" Mike Fink, won so many rifle shoots that he was barred from later contests.

One bloody diversion, cockfighting, became popular in the Bluegrass, but was later prohibited by law. The Bell County handlers below exhibit their prize cocks.

© 1968 *Saturday Evening Post*

After the Civil War, almost every village had a baseball team that played on Sunday afternoons in converted cow pastures. In 1876 Louisville became the birthplace of the National League. The city's team later switched to the Federal League, from which the American League developed, and stayed in the majors until 1899.

Among Kentucky's "big name" players were Earle Combs of the New York Yankees (above, left) and Peewee Reese of the Brooklyn Dodgers. Combs in 1970 was elected to the Baseball Hall of Fame and was honored at a banquet where he is shown above (wearing cap) with (from left): Jack McGrath, Frank McMenamin, Jack Hillerich, Bill Becker, and Combs's Yankee teammates of the 1920s "Pat" Olsen and Joe Sewell.

Football and baseball were the major sports at the University of Kentucky until around the turn of the century, when basketball began to attract fans. When the 1912 team (left) won the championships of Kentucky and (unofficially) of the South, basketball was the second favorite sport at UK. It was eventually to overshadow both football and baseball.

In 1921, the first collegiate basketball champions of the South posed with their coach, George Buchheit (left, back row), after capturing the title on a rattling, temporary court in Atlanta. Bill King, with the silver cup, made the winning free throw after time had expired.

Women played basketball from its inception in Kentucky. Sarah G. Blanding, later president of Vassar College, holding the ball, was captain of the 1924 girls' team at UK. Behind her is their coach, Albert B. "Happy" Chandler of Corydon, who was twice governor, United States Senator, and commissioner of baseball.

High schools have also taken to basketball, and the tournament today is one of the best attended in the nation, drawing around 170,000 fans annually.

In professional golf, Kentucky has had such champions as Marian Miley, Bobby Nichols, Gay Brewer, Jr., and Frank Beard.

Adolph Rupp, the "Baron of Basketball," has guided the Kentucky Wildcats to 858 victories with only 183 losses in a forty-one-year period from 1930 to 1971—a record for collegiate coaches.

Rupp and his "Fabulous Five" of 1947-1948 (top of page) were part of the United States squad which won the 1948 Olympic basketball title in London. From left are Ralph Beard, Kenny Rollins, Cliff Barker, Wallace Jones, and Alex Groza.

John Cox, with ball, and Vern Hatton led Kentucky's "Fiddlin' Five" (above) to the 1958 National Collegiate Athletic Association championship.

The late Ed Diddle, waving his famous red towel, coached Western Kentucky University basketball for forty-two years. Shown with his 1947-1948 squad, he compiled a record of 759 victories and 302 losses. In 1971 Western played in the NCAA tournament finals.

Co-captain of the 1936 UK tennis team, Elvis J. Stahr (right) became secretary of the army, president of Indiana University, and head of the National Audubon Society. E. T. "Ned" Breathitt, a UK track letterman, became governor of Kentucky.

NATIONAL CHAMPIONS 1921

First row, left to right: Dewey Kimbel, Hump Tanner, ...?, Case Thomasson, Tom Bartlett, Norris Armstrong (capt.), Terry Snowday, Bo McMillin, Joe Murphy, Jim Green. Second row, left to right: Minos Gordy, Ben Cregor, ...?, Buck Jones, R. M. Gibson, Ed Kubale, George Chinn, Bill Shadoan, Frank Rubarth, Bill James. Third row, left to right: Weldon Bradley, ...?, Bill Priest, ...?, Royce Flippin, George Jones, ..., ...?, Sheridan Ingerson, Leslie Combs. Fourth row: Tiny Thornhill, Tom Moran, S. Anderson, ...?, ...?, Coach Charlie Moran.

CENTRE 14	CLEMSON 0	CENTRE 6	HARVARD 0	CENTRE 21	TULANE 0
CENTRE 14	VPI 0	CENTRE 55	KENTUCKY 0	CENTRE 38	ARIZONA 0
CENTRE 28	XAVIER 0	CENTRE 21	AUBURN 0	CENTRE 14	TEXAS A&M 21
CENTRE 98	TRANSY. 0	CENTRE 25	W&L 0		

Football also had its moments of glory in Kentucky, notably with Centre College in the 1920s and with the University of Kentucky just after World War II.

The "Praying Colonels" of Centre captured the imagination of the country when, coached by Charley Moran, they defeated Harvard 6 to 0 in the "upset of the century" in 1921. Leaders of the team were (from left) Bo McMillan, "Red" Roberts, and Captain Norris "Army" Armstrong. Centre had played another game with Harvard the year before and had lost 31-14.

During an eight-year reign (1946-1953), Paul "Bear" Bryant coached the UK Wildcats to sixty wins, twenty-three losses, and five ties.

Vito "Babe" Parilli, All-American quarterback, carries the ball above as UK defeats Oklahoma 13-7 in the 1951 Sugar Bowl. The next year Kentucky upset T.C.U., 20-7, in the Cotton Bowl.

Louisville's Cassius Clay (Muhammad Ali) successfully defended his heavyweight title in a return match with deposed champion Sonny Liston in 1965. Ali kept his crown from 1964 to 1968. Two other Kentuckians, also from Louisville, have held the world's heavyweight championship: Marvin Hart, 1905-1906, and James Ellis, 1968-1970.

XVI. THE HORSE

Near the frontier community of Lexington the first race path in Kentucky was marked in an attempt to banish the rowdy frontier custom of racing horses on the town streets. These races, run without rules or much regard for the safety of bystanders, became such a nuisance that the legislature forbade the practice in town charters granted after 1810.

By this time the thoroughbred industry was well-established in the central Bluegrass region. Kentucky breeders were building equine dynasties, and good stallions, among them Henry Clay's Buzzard, were at a premium.

In the 1830s, Kentucky began to challenge the leadership of the older breeding and racing centers in New York, tidewater Virginia, Mississippi, South Carolina, and New Orleans. Woodburn Farm near Versailles in Woodford County became one of the leading stock farms in the nation. And the per-

formance of Bluegrass horses in the famous Angora-Randolph and Grey Eagle-Wagner matches in this period spread the fame of the Kentucky runner.

Oakland Course at Louisville (below, left) was the site of the Grey Eagle-Wagner races in 1839. Lodging in Oakland House, at the entrance gate, was available to patrons.

THE FULL BLOODED HORSE
PAYMASTER,

WILL stand the ensuing season at Baron Court House to cover ___ at fifteen dollars the season, which may be discharged with the payment of ___, Beef cattel or pork on foot, delivered at John Mayfield's cotton Gin by the ___ day of December next, at their market prices : ten dollars cash will discharge each season if paid by the first day of July, eight dollars the single leap, which must be paid when the mare is covered, thirty dollars to insure a colt provided the mare is not parted with. Notes will be required of those who puts mares, and gentlemen living at a distance that sends mares will be so kind as to send attested notes along with them.

PAYMASTER was imported from England by col. Parker of New-York at two years and ten months old, is a beautiful chenut brown with black legs, about sixteen hands high, eleven yeas old, free from blemish of any kind. Much might be said of the lofty commanding figure, elegant proportion, bone, power and activity this Horse possesses, but a better recommendation of him is that gentlemen should view and examine him.

PAYMASTER was got by King Furgus (the sire of Hambletonian and Bingsborough at this time the best runing horse in Europe.) his grand sire Felps his great grand sire Mark &c. &c his dam by Fortitude., his grand dam by Squirrel, his great gr. dam by Regulus, his great great gr. dam by Logsdale, Bay Arabian's Bevereleys Turk &c. &c. &c. Pasture will be provided for mares coming from a distance at the customary prices. The greatest care will be taken but we will not be liable for escapes or accident's. The season will commence the 10th of March, and end the 1st, day of July.

RICHARD BOHANNON,
WILLIAM VERNOUGHT.

Jefferson 18th, Feb'y, 1807.
N. B. The Alston Colt will also be let to mares at the same stand, where the terms will be made known.
B. & V.

WE whose names are under wriitten do certify, that we are acquainted with the horse called Paymaster, the property of Mr. Vernought, and that he was accounted a sure foal getter, and that the mares have proved with foal a greater number than from any horse that was let to such a number of mares.

Given under our hands this 9th, day of Feb'y, 1807.
The above certificate is true as to my mares.

Thos. Sanders   Rob. Lucky
Jas. Earickson   Joseph Simmons
Fred. Hinderlighter Henry Field.

FIRST RACE COURSE

NEAR THIS SPOT PIONEERS IN 1780, ESTABLISHED THE STARTING POINT OF THE FIRST RACE PATH IN KENTUCKY, EXTENDING SOUTHWARD ONE QUARTER MILE.

—HISTORICAL MARKERS SOCIETY—

Boston (above), the sire of Lexington, was one of the most exciting of early American racers. Foaled in 1833, Boston raced through the age of ten, winning forty of forty-five starts.

No other horse has sired as many brilliant runners as did Lexington (right). His offspring included Kentucky (lower left), Asteroid (lower right), and Preakness, after which the famous Maryland stakes are named. Each was among the best runners of the latter half of the nineteenth century.

Famous Kentucky stallions of more recent times include such proud names as Bull Lea, Bold Ruler, Man o' War, Nashua, and Hail to Reason. In the 1960s Bold Ruler was the leading American sire for seven years, a record surpassed only by Lexington.

Lexington's career brought such renown to the city for which he was named that in 1854 the citizens presented the elaborately engraved punchbowl (right) to his owner, Dr. Elisha Warfield. The "Lexington Bowl," fashioned by local silversmiths, was given to the Keeneland Association after its opening in 1936 and was for many years the trophy awarded the winner of the annual Bluegrass Stakes in Lexington.

The Lexington Trots Breeders' Association track (Red Mile) now has replaced the old grandstand and trotting track shown here in the late 1880s or early 1890s.

The Kentucky horse Grey Eagle (left) met the highly regarded Tennessee-bred Wagner in the fall of 1839. At their first race on September 30 about 10,000 people—half the population of Louisville at the time—turned out to watch Wagner win all three heats by narrow margins. Both horses earlier had been entered in the Jockey Club Purse, run on October 5. The first heat of that race was won by Grey Eagle, the second by Wagner. In the final trial Grey Eagle was lamed before he finished the course.

The jockey field at first was dominated by Negroes. Oliver Lewis, a Negro jockey, piloted Aristides (below) to fame in the first Kentucky Derby in 1875.

Most famous of these jockeys was Isaac Murphy (left), the first to ride three horses to victory in the Kentucky Derby:

The king of American thoroughbreds, Man o' War appears as a two-year-old (right).

In his redoubtable career he lost only once out of twenty-one starts, that time in 1919 to a horse appropriately named Upset. In 1920 he won two notable victories—an $80,000 match race against Sir Barton and the Dwyer Stakes. In the latter race John P. Grier ran neck and neck with him for over a mile, but "Big Red" moved out to win (above). His two racing seasons netted his owner Samuel Riddle about $250,000 at a time when purses were not so large.

Although he never raced in Kentucky, "Big Red" retired to stud at Riddle's Faraway Farm near Lexington. Here his groom Will Harbut's colorful stories of "de mostest hoss" helped make him the leading tourist attraction of the Bluegrass.

When Man o' War died at the age of thirty in November 1947, several thousand attended the funeral. A heroic-sized statue (right) marks his grave in Man o' War Park.

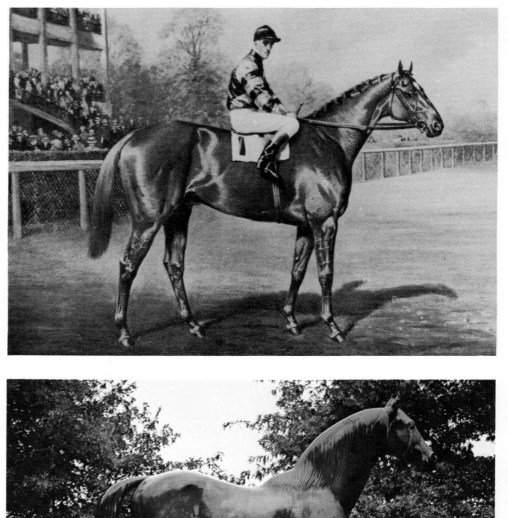

The first horse cemetery in Kentucky (above, right) is located on the old John Harper farm near Midway in Woodford County. The markers recall the great Longfellow, a leading American sire of the 1870s, and Ten Broeck.

Regret, the only filly to win the Kentucky Derby (1915), helped bring national attention to the race. Her owner, H. P. Whitney, sent the undefeated filly (above) to Churchill Downs as the most prestigious eastern runner to venture "West."

The first Derby winner (1917) not foaled in the United States was the English-bred Omar Khayyam (below). Not until 1959 did another foreign-bred horse, Tomy Lee, win the Run for the Roses.

Among the great runners produced in Kentucky is Whirlaway (left), bred by the famous Calumet Farm near Lexington. Twice named Horse of the Year, he won the Triple Crown—the Kentucky Derby, the Preakness and Belmont Stakes. The first horse to win $500,000 on the track, Whirlaway sired seventeen stakes winners.

Nashua was known for his tendency to wait until the final furlongs before making his move to the front. He was upset in the 1955 Kentucky Derby by Swaps, but later evened the record by defeating his competitor in a celebrated match race in Chicago. Nashua was the first horse to bring a $1,000,000 sale price, a figure which would be modest today.

Nashua, with Eddie Arcaro up (middle, left) enters the track at Keeneland near Lexington for a farewell exhibition gallop before retiring in 1956 to Leslie Combs II's Spendthrift Farm. Combs is shown walking behind Nashua.

Probably the greatest horse since Man o' War, Citation was the first thoroughbred to earn $1,000,000 and the last horse—in 1948—to have won the Triple Crown. He is shown (lower left) setting a world record of 1:33 3/5 for a mile at Golden Gate Fields.

Another Kentucky horse, Sir Barton, was the first to gain the Triple Crown. As a three-year-old he had never won a race but took the Kentucky Derby in 1919. Unsuccessful at stud, he died in 1937 at a western army station.

The Kentucky Derby is finished in a little over two minutes of actual running time except for the awarding of a trophy and the traditional blanket of red roses. But for thousands of fans who have witnessed the drama in historic Churchill Downs the race is relived in memory for years to come.

It all began May 17, 1875, when a chestnut colt, Aristides, came in first in a field of fourteen. That Derby was the second race on the opening day at the first meet at the new Jockey Club track in Louisville. Since then the event has become known as the world's greatest spectacle in thoroughbred racing.

First jewel in racing's Triple Crown, the Derby brings the nation's finest thoroughbreds to compete in a grueling mile and a quarter. Preceding the event are lavish parties and on the day itself a customary Derby breakfast.

Talk at the twin-spired Downs (right) is all of the winner. The spectators bandy about track records, owners, trainers, jockeys, and just plain hunches, but only one knows the answer—and that is the horse.

The excitement mounts from the time the horses and jockeys leave the enclosed paddock. Ten minutes before race time, they enter the fenced path to the track (opposite page, upper left), cheered on by well-wishers. The bands play "My Old Kentucky Home" as the hopefuls step onto the track, and the voices of over 100,000 spectators join in that sentimental tribute to the Bluegrass state.

The horses are in the starting gate—and then they're off. Fortunes, large and small, depend on the outcome of this classic. In terms of prestige, winning the Kentucky Derby is priceless. Even if his entry trails the field, the owner will ever after identify this particular animal as "my Derby horse."

Three-year-olds are nominated for the Derby on the basis of pedigree and past performances on the track. Many owners in futile attempts to capture the Derby trophy, have spent thousands.

The grandstand and clubhouse at historic Churchill Downs are the background for the field of contenders (lower left) as they round the first turn. The jockeys wear distinctively colored silk jackets and caps, provided by the horses' owners. Colors of the individual stables are registered with the Jockey Club and the State Racing Commission.

In a little over two minutes the race is over as horses thunder across the finish line (above). The winner's circle, and the traditional blanket of red roses, await the victor.

Thoroughbred sales in Lexington are attended by buyers from all over the world.

A record price for a yearling was set at Keeneland in 1970 when $510,000 was paid for a full brother to 1969 Derby and Preakness winner Majestic Prince. George Swinebroad (right), noted auctioneer, calls for a higher bid than the posted $500,000. Below, the asked-for amount is received and registered on the sale board. Flanking Swinebroad are auctioneer Tom Caldwell and pedigree announcer J. B. Faulconer.

Future champions can sell for considerably less. Cañonero II, winner of the 1971 Derby and Preakness, brought only $1200 as a yearling.

Standardbred or harness horses were not popular in early Kentucky because of poor roads. Organized breeding began at Robert A. Alexander's Woodburn Farm in Woodford County, but did not fully develop until after the Civil War.

The Kentucky-bred Greyhound (upper left) is shown in 1940 just before he sped an exhibition mile at Lexington's Red Mile track in 2:01 3/4, the fastest mile ever trotted under saddle. He was ridden —for the first time in his life— by the late Frances Dodge Van Lennep.

One of harness racing's most memorable performers, Greyhound in 1938 set a one-mile world record of 1:55 1/4 at the Red Mile with Sep Palin in the sulky, a record that stood until the 1968 Futurity winner Nevele Pride bettered it.

The Red Mile at Lexington, one of the eight tracks on harness racing's Grand Circuit, is known as the world's fastest harness track. More than 700 two-minute miles have been run on it. At the spring and fall meets the country's leading trotters compete for purses worth over $350,000.

Wing Commander (middle left, with Earl Teater up) was one of the all-time great show horse champions. The five-gaited stallion stood at Castleton Farm until his death at the age of twenty-six in 1969.

Jumpers are also raised in Kentucky. The one at left is clearing a steeplechase hurdle.

There are several breeds that are distinctively American, and one of them—the saddle horse—originated and developed in Kentucky. The first saddle horses were often used for common work. Not until later were finer, easy gaited animals bred.

The country fairs and horse shows that sprang up early in the state's history had considerable influence on improving the saddle horse. Horse shows in Kentucky today continue to encourage the best in equine performance and breeding. Above is a winner at the World Championship Horse Show at the Kentucky State Fair in Louisville.

The harness horses below are shown with high-wheeled sulkies.

Bluegrass pasturage, rich in lime, will create in the foal above the light strong bones and tendons necessary for a champion runner.

Good Counsel (below, left) was the fastest two-year-old filly pacer of all time. She was bred, raced and served as a broodmare for Castleton Farm near Lexington. Good Counsel set world records of 1:58.1 for the mile as a two-year-old and 1:57 at three, winning all the major stakes against colts and fillies alike. Speedy Scot (below, right) at three trotted a world record 1:56.4. Also a Castleton Farm horse, Speedy Scot won the 1963 Hambletonian and the Kentucky Futurity at the Red Mile in Lexington.

On picturesque Bluegrass farms like the one above, many of the finest thoroughbreds in the United States have been born. The awkward foal may be a winner someday, but first he must complete a rigorous training program in which he will be carefully watched for promising traits. He seems to have learned one of his first lessons already—to follow a lead. Later he will be taught to wear a bit and bridle, a blanket, girth, and saddle. Finally he will carry a rider. Gallops about the pasture or on the track will increase stamina, sprints will develop his natural speed. If he completes the preparatory schooling satisfactorily, he will enter his first race as a two-year-old.

XVII. LIVING IN THE GRAND MANNER

THOSE with the means to live well in Kentucky blended the aristocratic tradition of their eastern background with a robust ebullience natural to a land that was the nation's first frontier. They perpetuated the social institutions of the older states, including the practice of dueling.

When a person was challenged and refused to "give satisfaction," he was "posted," as the term went. Handbills were tacked up about town proclaiming the cowardice of the defaulter.

General Andrew Jackson and Charles Dickinson, both of Nashville, were the principals in one of the most famous duels in Kentucky on May 30, 1806, at Harrison's Mills on Red River in Logan County. Dickinson, although a crack shot, was killed. General Jackson's dueling pistols are shown below.

TO THE PUCLIC.

IN consideration of the gross and impudent falsehood of that part of the handbill of Martin H. Wickliff, just published against Thomas Speed, which has reference to me, the public are presented with the following document, which passed a few days after the encounter alluded to by Wickliff, and consequently must be numbered among the *civilities* received from me since that date.

Upon the authority of this document, I thus publicly proclaim Martin Hardin Wickliff, a gasconading cowardly poltroon and lying scoundrel, unworthy the notice or credit of any but persons as base and contemptible as himself.

BURR HARRISON.

October 20, 1819.

————

MARTIN H. WICKLIFF,

SIR—Our differences require an effectual termination; are you willing, for that purpose, to appeal to the mode settled and sanctioned by Gentlemen; or are you resolved to retreat for safety behind the municipal law.

My friend, Major Rector, who bears this, will receive your answer.

BURR HARRISON.

Sept. 5th, 1815.

————

I CERTIFY the above to be a true copy of the r   I handed to said Wickliff.
N. RECTOR.

Sept. 5th, 1815.

————

THE answer of Capt. M. H. Wickliff to the within note was, "I will have nothing to do with it, I told the Doctor so, and he knows it. I have taken several oaths against it and could not meet him in that way without *confiscating my property*," &c. My real opinion is, on my honor, I think Capt. M. H. Wickliff is lacking in courage, and think men would be in eminent danger to be commanded by him in the field of battle, as he must possess very feeble nerves indeed to swallow such a communication without replying to it, as an officer and soldier ought.

N. RECTOR.

TO THE WORLD!!

AUSTIN B. WICKHAM,

Having resorted to low, cowardly and dishonorable means, for the purpose of injuring my character and standing, and having refused honorable satisfaction, which I have demanded; I avail myself of this opportunity of publishing him to the world as a reclaimless liar, an infamous scoundrel, a black hearted villian, an arrant coward, a worthless vagabond and an imported miscreant, a base poltroon and a dishonor to his country.

PARIS, JUNE 23, 1848

WILLIAM B. VICTOR

Two of the leading figures of the American turf were Harry Payne Whitney and James Robert Keene, shown here at a race meeting shortly after the turn of the century. Keene (right) owner of Castleton Farm, was born in 1838 in London, England. He was owner of Sysonby and Colin, which are listed with Man o' War and Citation as the four greatest thoroughbreds of the twentieth century.

Whitney (left) the utility magnate who with his son C. V. Whitney operated the famous Greentree Farm near Lexington, was the owner of Regret, the only filly ever to win the Kentucky Derby.

Sally Ward (1827-1896) was a Louisville belle of the southern tradition, famed for her beauty, spirit, and wit.

During the summer, Kentuckians of means went to the many mineral springs, or spas, in the Commonwealth. Some guests came to "take the waters"; others sought refuge from the yellow fever of the Deep South. But most came for the social whirl which usually lasted from June through September at resorts such as Tatham Springs on Chaplin River in Washington County (below, opposite page) and the New Century Hotel (above) at Dawson Springs, Hopkins County.

Here, numerous marriages were arranged between the sons and daughters of wealthy Kentucky families and those from the Deep South. Economic ties, too, were forged. Springs were still popular in the 1890s to 1900s (below).

Field stone fences (upper right and right), laid without mortar, usually by slaves, were often used to enclose lush pastures and fields in the Bluegrass, where they are a familiar sight today. These were photographed in Fayette County.

The "lazy" gate (below) can be opened or closed without dismounting from a horse or leaving a vehicle. Manufactured in Lexington, it is also known as a "patent" or easy gate.

The meat log, or salt box (above, left), was made from a single poplar tree and is three feet in diameter and sixteen feet long. It was made about 1800 and used by a Hawesville family in Hancock County for many years to cure their meats.

Steamboats plying the Kentucky, Ohio, and Mississippi rivers sported luxurious accommodations. Travelers enjoyed the pleasures of a lavish table and whiled away the hours with dancing and various forms of entertainments.

In the spring, Kentucky thoroughbreds, their owners, and racing fans traveled south by boat to the race meets at Natchez and New Orleans. The packet's cargo usually included tobacco, wheat, cotton bagging, rope, corn, and meats destined for southern markets.

The *Belle of Louisville* (above), one of the last steamboats operating on the Ohio River, recaptures some of the color of the past century on daily summer cruises. During Derby Week the *Belle* races the *Delta Queen,* a rival boat from Cincinnati.

Five presidents of the United States—William Henry Harrison, James Monroe, Andrew Jackson, Zachary Taylor, and William Howard Taft—and numerous other famous persons, including the Marquis de Lafayette, have been welcomed in the reception room (above) at the old Governor's Mansion in Frankfort.

The chandelier and candelabra in the state dining room (right) were originally owned by Brutus Clay, son of Cassius Marcellus Clay. They once graced his home, Lynwood, in Richmond, Madison County.

Twin drawing rooms flank the main entrance to the mansion. In the photograph below may be seen one of two mantels made of Kentucky yellow poplar. The drawing rooms are furnished with many rare antiques.

Antebellum Southerners delighted in an extravagant display of wealth, particularly when entertaining, and the prosperous landlords, lawyers, and merchants of the Bluegrass were no exceptions. In 1796, Colonel David Meade left his tidewater estate in Virginia to build Chaumière du Prairie in Jessamine County. Many prominent visitors came to meet Chaumière's courtly host and to admire his hundred-acre lawn, lakes, bridges, and splendid pagodas. At a Christmas dinner in 1818, Colonel Meade seated one hundred guests.

Not every host could approach the elegant standards of Chaumière, but many entertained handsomely. The John Rowan home, Federal Hill, in Bardstown (above), once was the scene of much lavish hospitality, such as the reenactment above.

XVIII. KENTUCKY TODAY

LEGEND

1 Abraham Lincoln Birthplace National Historic Site.	15 Cumberland Gap National Historical Park.
2 Ballard County Wildlife Management Area.	16 Dale Hollow Lake.
3 Barren River Lake State Resort Park.	17 Daniel Boone National Forest.
4 Bernheim and Knobs State Forest.	Daniel Boone Hut—Gray's Arch
5 Big Bone Lick State Park.	Hoedown Island—Natural Bridge
6 Blue Licks Battlefield State Park.	Pioneer Weapons Hunting Area
7 Breaks Interstate Park.	Red River Gorge—Sky Bridge
☆ Buckhorn Lake State Resort Park.	18 Dewey Lake State Forest.
9 Cane Ridge Shrine.	19 Dr. Thomas Walker State Shrine.
☆ Carter Caves State Resort Park.	20 Duncan Tavern.
11 Columbus-Belmont Battlefield State Park.	21 Fishtrap Lake.
12 Constitution Square State Shrine.	22 Fort Boonesborough State Park.
13 Cranks Creek Wildlife Management Area.	23 Frankfort, Kentucky.
	Old State House—State Capitol Building
	Buckley—Audubon Wildlife Refuge
☆ Cumberland Falls State Resort Park.	24 General Burnside State Park (Chandler Island).
	☆ General Butler State Resort Park.

KENTUCKY has a vigorous tradition extending back to Daniel Boone's first visit in 1767, but tradition has not withstood sweeping winds of change as the twentieth century gathered momentum. The swift pace of technology, the growth of mass media, and the building of a great highway system to connect once-isolated sections with the rest of the Commonwealth and the nation, have had their effects. Kentucky has also been required to make great advances in education in order to prepare her young people to meet the challenges of a rapidly evolving society.

Nevertheless, the power and color of Kentucky's past continue to shape the course of her present. The emotional orientation toward the agrarian life, the tradition of hospitality and tolerance, the love for nature and for politics—all are displayed in the vitality and survival of institutions such as county fairs and the horse and tobacco industries.

The Kentuckian's love of the land is displayed in a distinguished state park system—the leading one in the United States—and other outdoor recreation facilities including historic sites and shrines. Within the park system, efforts are being made to preserve wildlife and natural beauty.

The state park network is complemented by Land Between the Lakes, a national land and water development project in western Kentucky; the Daniel Boone National Forest and Red River Gorge; and many private and public outdoor recreational and monument areas.

The Breaks of Sandy, in Pike County, are at right. Lake Barkley State Resort Park, far right.

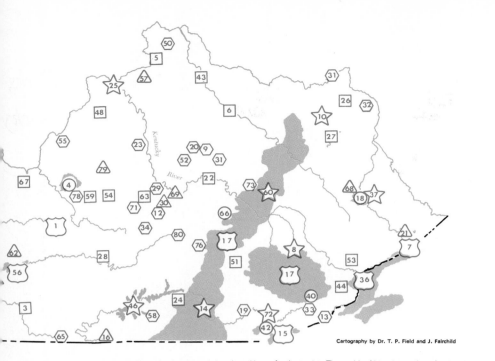

Cartography by Dr. T. P. Field and J. Fairchild

As Kentucky was a Mecca for the pioneer it is today a Mecca for the tourist. The wealth of historic, scenic and water recreation resources have been enhanced by the development of extensive and attractive facilities for visitors. In fully half of the state parks the visitor has a complete range of vacation accommodations available. Because of the excellent highway network, which combines the Interstate system with the state Parkway system, all recreational facilities are within an easy day's drive of each other.

Doctor Thomas Walker, venturing into the wilderness in 1750, entered Kentucky through the gap which he named for the Duke of Cumberland. The overlook from the Pinnacle at Cumberland Gap is shown above.

Formed by exposure for centuries to the erosion of wind and rain, Balanced Rock in the Red River Gorge is one of the natural formations accessible to hikers on trails in the Daniel Boone National Forest. The forest, managed by the United States Forest Service in the Department of Agriculture, includes over 575,000 acres in the rolling foothills of the Cumberland Plateau. These lands are open to the public for hunting, fishing, and camping.

There are other caves in the vicinity of Mammoth Cave, but this geological attraction is one of the seven natural wonders of the world. The full extent of its limestone caverns is still not determined, and new areas are opened to visitors each year.

Mammoth Cave National Park includes over 50,000 acres in south-central Kentucky and is managed by the National Park Service.

Along the underground passageways are such views as famed Crystal Lake (left) and the Rotunda.

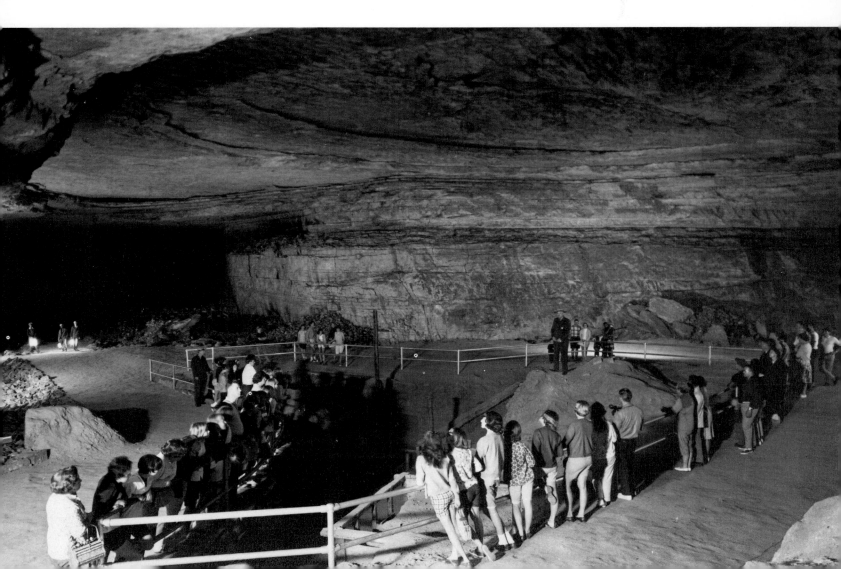

Kentucky's lakes and streams provide opportunity for all kinds of water-related recreation. Dale Hollow Reservoir is the home of bass, crappie, trout, bream, and walleye.

The Land Between the Lakes recreation and conservation area (below) contains more surface acres of water than of land. The primary purpose of building the reservoir was to develop flood control and to generate electric power, but the vacation advantages for Kentuckians and other tourists have become major benefits.

Cumberland Falls, the Niagara of the South, is located in Cumberland Falls State Resort Park, eighteen miles southwest of Corbin.

Kentucky is second only to Alaska among the states in miles of running streams.

From 1960 to 1971, the number of state parks increased from twenty-three to thirty-five. The park system includes vacation resorts such as the lodges and recreation areas at Lakes Barkley and Cumberland, as well as historic shrines from my Old Kentucky Home at Bardstown to the site of Fort Boonesborough on the banks of the Kentucky River.

The lodge at Pennyrile State Park (above, left).

Castle Rock, once a well-known rendezvous for Kentucky pioneers is on Rockcastle River, in Rockcastle County (above, right).

Wolf Creek Dam, just south of Jamestown, impounds the Cumberland River to form Lake Cumberland.

Chain Rock at Pine Mountain State Resort Park in eastern Kentucky (left).

A typical white board fence seen on many Bluegrass horse farms (below, left).

Native wild turkeys in Land Between the Lakes in western Kentucky (below).

Spindletop at Lexington, an independent, non-profit applied research institute chartered in 1961, is devoted to development of improved technological methods for industry and government. Governor Louie B. Nunn, shown in front of the build-ing, is one of the directors and supporters of this agency.

Jim Host, former state Parks Commissioner, announces the opening of Barren River State Resort Park near Glasgow.

Horses, the "crop" for which Bluegrass farms are most famous.

The United States Gold Depository at Fort Knox, south of Louisville. Completed in 1937, the fortified bullion vault houses the major portion of gold reserve of the United States.

Old slave-built fence on Shady Lane on the Old Frankfort Pike between Lexington and Frankfort.

The Physiographic Regions of Kentucky

After N. M. Fenneman

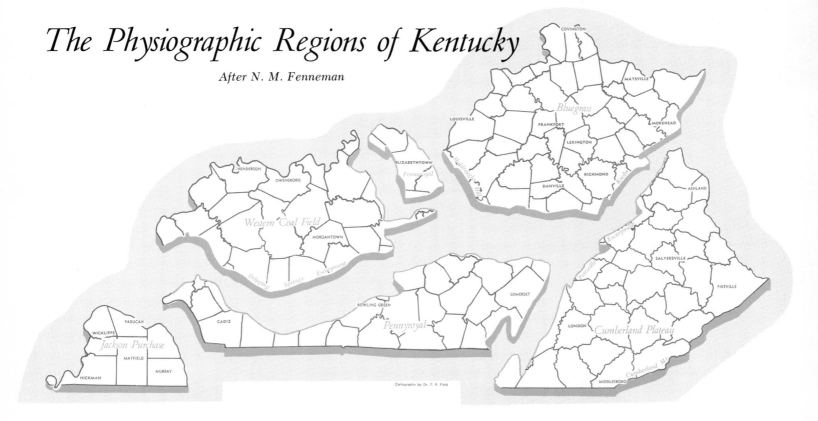

COVINGTON
MAYSVILLE
Bluegrass
LOUISVILLE
FRANKFORT
MOREHEAD
LEXINGTON
RICHMOND
DANVILLE
HENDERSON
OWENSBORO
ELIZABETHTOWN
Pennyroyal
ASHLAND
Western Coal Field
MORGANTOWN
SALYERSVILLE
Dripping Springs Escarpment
PIKEVILLE
PADUCAH
BOWLING GREEN
SOMERSET
WICKLIFFE
CADIZ
Pennyroyal
Cumberland Plateau
Jackson Purchase
LONDON
MAYFIELD
MURRAY
HICKMAN
MIDDLESBORO

Cartography by Dr. T. P. Field

Kentucky's physiographic regions are parts of the three great physiographic divisions of the eastern United States. Their contrasting qualities enter into the state's great variety.

North of Henderson is John James Audubon State Park which contains 590 acres of woods, a bird sanctuary, lake, nature center, and museum. The artist lived in this area for a number of years.

Among the natural beauties of Kentucky are the many species of wild-flowers. On this page, from left: butterfly weed, or orange milkweed; painted trillium; and columbine.

The rare yellow lady's-slipper or moccasin-flower.

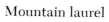

Spiderwort

Birdfoot violet

Mountain laurel

These symbolic scenes of harvest and the Christmas tree at the State Capitol mark year's end for Kentuckians — and close this panorama of a state rich in tradition and history.

KENTUCKY
As originally mapped by John Filson

This is the first—and most famous—map of Kentucky. It appeared in John Filson's book, *The Discovery, Settlement and Present State of Kentucke*, published by James Adams in 1784 at Wilmington, Delaware. It is generally believed that the map was also printed separately for sale to emigrants leaving for the Western Country. The map went through some seven or eight printings, each having only minor changes made on the original copper plate engraved by Henry D. Pursell at Philadelphia and printed by T. Rook for inclusion in the book. The watermark on the original map shows a plow with the words: WORK & BE RICH.